Austrian Country Inns
& Castles

BOOKS IN KAREN BROWN'S COUNTRY INN SERIES

Austrian Country Inns & Castles

English, Welsh & Scottish Country Inns

European Country Cuisine - Romantic Inns & Recipes

European Country Inns - Best on a Budget

French Country Inns & Chateaux

German Country Inns & Castles

Irish Country Inns

Italian Country Inns & Villas

Portuguese Country Inns & Pousadas

Scandinavian Country Inns & Manors

Spanish Country Inns & Paradors

Swiss Country Inns & Chalets

Austrian Country Inns & Castles

CLARE BROWN

Illustrated by

BARBARA TAPP

Karen Brown's Country Inn Series

WARNER BOOKS

Travel Press editors: Clare Brown, CTC, Karen Brown,
June Brown, CTC, Kirsten Price, Iris Sandilands

Illustrations and cover painting: Barbara Tapp
Maps: Keith Cassell

This book is written in cooperation with:
Town and Country - Hillsdale Travel
16 East Third Avenue, San Mateo, California 94401

Warner Books Edition
Copyright © 1986, 1988 by Travel Press
This Warner Books edition is published by arrangement with
Travel Press, San Mateo, California 94401

Warner Books, Inc., 666 Fifth Avenue, New York, NY 10103
Ⓦ A Warner Communications Company

Printed in the United States of America
First Warner Trade Paperback Printing: April 1988
10 9 8 7 6 5 4 3 2 1

LIBRARY OF CONGRESS
Library of Congress Cataloging-in-Publication Data

Brown, Karen.
    Austrian country inns and castles / Karen Brown.
        p.   cm.
    Rev. ed. of: Austrian country inns & castles / Clare Brown. c1986
    Includes indexes.
ISBN 0-446-38812-2 (pbk.) (U.S.A.) / 0-446-38960-9(pbk.) (Canada)
    1. Hotels, taverns, etc. -- Austria -- Guide-books. 2.Castles-
-Austria -- Guide-books. 3. Austria--Description and travel--1981--
-Guide-books. I. Brown, Clare. Austrian country inns & castles.
II. Title.
TX910.A8B76 1988
647'.9443601--dc19
                                      87-27233
                                         CIP

To Steve

Thanks for Life

And Love of Travel

Contents

HOTEL SECTION

INDEX OF HOTELS

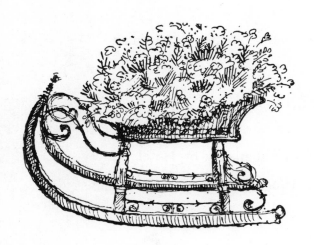

Introduction

GEMUTLICHKEIT - a favorite word of the Austrians. A word whose meaning conveys the essence of what makes Austria so very special - open friendliness, "olde worlde" charm, cozy ambiance, country simplicity and old fashioned hospitality: all the ingredients which make Austria a treasure just waiting to be discovered. The warmth of welcome and the Austrians' love of preserving the best of their heritage combine to produce a marvelous travel experience. Best of all, under this happy blanket of "gemutlichkeit" lies a fascinating country to visit. Many visitors see only Vienna, Salzburg, Innsbruck and perhaps Kitzbuhel - all wonderful towns. But the traveler who returns home without sampling more of this exquisite small country has definitely missed much that Austria has to offer. Read through this guide and see what you might miss. Allocate the time to venture away from the major tourist centers. You will be well rewarded. Live like royalty in a hilltop castle on the Hungarian border. Relax in an ancient farmhouse on the shores of the emerald-green Weissensee. Pretend you are a child again and revel in the delights of riding one of Austria's marvelous little narrow gauge toy-like trains. Slip into the depths of one of Austria's ancient salt mines on a wooden slide worn smooth as silk through years of use. Bring your skis and spend your winter holiday in a cozy chalet meeting the challenge of Europe's finest mountain slopes. Venture into immense ice caverns where soft lights play magic with the frozen fantasies. Pack your sturdy shoes and wander over well marked trails into hidden hamlets. Climb aboard an old-fashioned ferry and discover quaint villages tucked into tiny coves. Relax on a romantic castle terrace overlooking the Danube as you sip a superb local wine. Read on. The fantasyland of Austria awaits.

ABOUT THIS GUIDE

This guide is written with two main objectives: to describe the most charming, small, atmospheric hotels throughout Austria and to "tie" these hotels together with itineraries that include enough details so that the traveler can plan his own holiday.

Any guide which tries to be all things for all people fails. This guide does not try to give in-depth information on sightseeing - just highlights of some of the most tempting places to see. While traveling you will need to supplement this guide with a detailed reference such as Michelin's "Tourist Guide to Austria", an excellent, reliable source for addresses and dates and times museums are open. This guide does not try to give a complete listing of hotels in Austria, only the best. We have read guide books, magazines, newspaper articles and letters from our readers intensively. Every hotel that sounded as though it held a special appeal was contacted. After sorting through literally hundreds of brochures, the list was drastically cut to less than two hundred. These we personally visited and honed the final list down to just over sixty. In other words, we have done your homework for you.

This guide does not try to appeal to everyone. Tastes and preferences vary. This book is definitely prejudiced; the hotels included are ones we have seen and liked. It might be an elegant castle overlooking the Danube or a simple but romantic farmhouse nestled by a lake. But there is a common denominator - they all have charm. Our theory is that where you stay each night matters. Your hotels should add the touch of perfection that makes your holiday very special. The memories you bring home should be more than just of museums, theaters and tours through palaces. These are important but this guide takes you through the enchanting back roads of Austria and introduces you to the pleasure of staying in romantic hideaways.

CREDIT CARDS

Many small hotels do not accept credit cards.   Those hotels which do accept "plastic payment" are indicated in the hotel description section using the following abbreviations: AX - American Express, VS - Visa, MC - Master Charge, DC - Diner's Club, or simply - all major.

CURRENT

You will need a transformer plus an adapter if you plan to take an American made electrical appliance.   The voltage is 220 AC current at 50 cycles/second.   Check with the manager of the hotel before plugging anything into the outlet.

DRIVING

BELTS: Seat belts must be worn by everyone in the car.   Children under twelve must not sit in the front seat.

DRIVER'S LICENSE: Your local driver's license is accepted in Austria.   It must of course be current.   Many people prefer to travel with an International Driver's License which is always an excellent idea although not mandatory. The minimum driving age is eighteen.

DRUNK DRIVING: It is a very serious offence to drive when you have been drinking.   Anyone with an alcohol blood level of 0.8 % (less than two beers) is considered "under the influence", which is a serious offence.   Therefore, do not drink and drive - save your liquid refreshments for evening meals when your driving is finished for the day.

GASOLINE: Gasoline is very expensive so budget this as part of your trip if you are driving.   On an average, you will probably spend approximately $15.00 per day on gasoline.   In addition to the expected combinations of premium and standard gasolines, many stations have another choice where you can create your own mixture to arrive at the perfect octane combination for your car by adjusting the dial on the pump.

PARKING PERMITS: In some of the cities parking permits are needed for parking zones.   Cars parked in these special zones display in the front window a cardboard clock, available free at gasoline stations, banks, police stations and tobacco stores.   The system is to set the hands of the clock at the time you leave the car so that if a policeman comes by he can check that you have not overstayed your time.   Some cities have a slightly different system: instead of free paper clocks, you must buy a voucher which you display on the dashboard to be readable through the front window.

ROADS: Most of the major cities are connected by expressways which are marked by signs showing a double blue line.   Traffic moves fast on the expressways where there is a speed limit of 80 miles or 130 kilometers per hour.   Highways are also excellent roads, and complete the network.   The joy of traveling on these roads is that there is relatively little traffic.   Of course, the stream of cars increases as you approach major cities, but compared with other European countries the roads are blissfully tranquil.   It is rare to be delayed behind a line of cars or a stream of slow moving trucks.   Not to say though that you might not have to wait while a line of cows meander across the road on their way home from pasture or slow down for a few miles while a farmer drives his tractor back to the farm.   The speed limit on these roads is 62 miles or 100 kilometers per hour.   In towns the limit is 31 miles or 50 kilometers per hour.

ROAD SIGNS: Before starting on the road, prepare yourself by learning the international driving signs so that you can obey all the rules of the road and avoid the embarrassment of heading the wrong way down a small street or parking in a forbidden area! There are several basic sign shapes. The triangular signs warn that there is danger ahead. The circular signs indicate compulsory rules and information. The square signs give information concerning telephones, parking, camping, etc. Some of the more common signs are listed below.

End of all restrictions | Halt sign | Halt sign | Customs | No stopping | No parking/waiting

Mechanical help | Filling station | Telephone | Camping site | Caravan site | Youth hostel

All vehicles prohibited | No entry for all vehicles | No right turn | No U-turns | No entry for motorcars | No overtaking

Road works | Loose chippings | Level crossing with barrier | Level crossing without barrier | Maximum speed limit | End of speed limit

Traffic signals ahead | Pedestrians | Children | Animals | Wild animals | Other dangers

Introduction

FOOD

Food in Austria is *NOT* a problem unless you are watching your waistline. You can eat any time, anywhere: it is amazing. Small cafes are found along seemingly deserted mountain paths. Warming huts serving an assortment of hot mulled wine, cider, crepes, sausages, soups and sandwiches are strategically positioned to tempt skiers in from their mountain descent. Even the smallest town is liberally sprinkled with restaurants. In summer sidewalk terraces magically blossom with tables set with jaunty umbrellas. When you visit Austria prepare to eat, and eat well.

Breakfast usually consists of a buffet of cheeses, cold meats, cereal, breads, butter, homemade jams, juice and pate, along with a choice of coffee, tea, or hot chocolate. Mid morning it is tempting to stop for coffee and one of Austria's delectable pastries, then only a few hours after lunch the cafes are busy serving tea and strudel. It is stylish to linger in a coffee house to watch the people and have an ice cream.

Generally the food is excellent. Most countryside inns cultivate small gardens which provide the delicious salads and vegetables. Jams are often homemade, breads usually fresh from the oven. The hotel owners are frequently the chefs, and if not, closely supervise the preparation of food. Forget your diet, "Mit Schlag" (with cream) is the byword in Austria and far too good to pass up. The Austrians use cream on everything - even meat. All your walking will easily compensate for a little indulgence.

A unique Austrian institution is the Coffee House. It seems that when the Turks were finally ousted from Austria, in their haste to flee, they left many supplies, including bags of the precious coffee bean. Quick to capitalize on a free gift, an enterprising Viennese learned how to prepare his bounty and opened the first Viennese coffee house. Soon the rage spread and coffee houses sprouted up all over the city. The coffee, although superb and served in an astonishingly creative number of ways, is really only incidental: the coffee house serves as a club where friends meet, play chess, read the paper, or just sit and think. Newspapers and magazines are stretched on wooden hangers to be perused leisurely, and games are stacked on shelves and may be borrowed. The coffee is expensive, but not when you realize what an assortment of pleasures are purchased with one small cup.

Austria is surrounded by seven countries - Germany, Switzerland, Liechtenstein, Italy, Yugoslavia, Hungary and Czechoslovakia. Therefore, it is not surprising that there is such a wonderful selection of cuisine. Austria has absorbed some of the best from each of her neighbors and, with tricks from the kitchen, giving them a uniquely Austrian touch. The following list includes some of Austria's most popular foods:

BACKHENDL - Young chickens, breaded and fried to a golden brown.

BREADS - There are too many varieties of delicious breads to list them. Most hotels and restaurants take pride in serving wonderful "home baked" breads.

BREGENZERWALD CHEESES - If you follow the "Marvelous Mountains of Tyrol and Vorarlberg" itinerary in this guide, you will travel through the little villages of the Bregenzerwald which produce delicious cheeses.

FRANKFURTERS - Contrary to what one would expect, these delicious little sausages originated in Vienna, not in Germany.

GAME - All kinds of game are served and understandably are the specialty of hotels that were once hunting lodges.

GULYAS - Goulash served both as a stew and also frequently as a soup - a hearty combination of onions and meat, heavily flavored with paprika.

KARFIOLSUPPE - A thick cauliflower soup.

KNODEL - A flour dumpling, flavored with spices and served instead of potatoes with meats, blended with pate and dropped into soups, stuffed with jam and fried, or filled with a sweet fruit and served for dessert.

KRAPFEN - A delicious pastry which is filled with a sweet fruit filling and then deep fried.

LEBERKNODELSUPPE - A delicious broth with a large pate-flavored dumpling floating in the middle.

PALATSCHINKEN - Thin pancakes sometimes rolled around, or stacked, with a filling such as hazelnuts and topped with whipped cream.

SALAT - Salad is usually a combination of sliced vegetables and greens. However, if you prefer, you can ask for "Gruner Salat" - green salad.

SALZBURGER NOCKERL - A souffle made from stiffly beaten eggs and a little flour, served piping hot from the oven and dusted with sugar.

SCHWAMMERLN GEBACKEN - Mushrooms dipped in batter and deep fried, served with a mayonnaise dill sauce.

STRUDEL - Pie-like pastries with a layered crust. There are many variations of this pastry, the most popular being apple strudel.

TAFELSPITZ - A large piece of beef simmered with herbs and wine until very tender, then sliced and served.

TIROLER GROSTL - Similar to what we call "hash". Cooked beef is cut into small pieces then fried with onions, potatoes and caraway seed.

TORTE - A layered cake with a wide choice of fillings. The most famous is the Sacher Torte, a chocolate cake filled with apricot jam and iced with chocolate.

WIENER SCHNITZEL - Thin filets of veal, dipped in egg and bread crumbs then fried to a golden brown.

ZWIEBELROSTBRATEN - Beef steaks which have been hammered thin and then quickly fried on both sides and served with sauteed onion.

HISTORY

Read some Austrian history before your holiday - it will make your sightseeing tingle with reality. The rows of portraits you will be seeing in museums will come to life with stories more romantic, more scandalous, more heartwarming than any modern soap opera. There are true stories to appeal to everyone. What, for example, could touch the soul of every modern woman more than the tale of marvelous Maria Theresa? In 1740, at the age of 23, she assumed the throne of Austria when her father, Charles VI, died unexpectedly. She had absolutely no training for the job and was considered easy prey by the eager politicians just waiting to gain control from this "chit of a girl". But she fooled them - and the world. Taking orders from no one, she revitalized the army, built a school system, established Vienna as the center of medicine, reformed the tax laws, created sound economic policies, and negotiated political agreements with neighboring countries - all achieved through a genius for negotiating, reckless courage and tremendous charm. During her reign, she laid the foundation upon which Austria continued to remain a dominant European power until the first part of the 20th century. Maria

Theresa accomplished these fabulous feats while ruling with integrity and compassion. She also raised twelve children (sixteen were born but four died in childhood) for whom she arranged royal marriages throughout Europe in hopes of bonding political alliances. The most famous of these arranged marriages was that of of her beautiful youngest daughter, Maria Antonia (later called Marie Antoinette), who at the age of fifteen was sent to France to marry the son of Louis XV - a marriage whose disastrous results is another chapter in history. Maria Theresa's story is just one of many equally enticing tales - read, enjoy, and be fortified with information which will add sparkle to your sightseeing.

HOTEL DESCRIPTIONS

This book is divided into two sections with hotel descriptions in both. The first portion of the book outlines itineraries and a hotel with a brief description is suggested for each destination. The second section of the book is a complete list of hotels, appearing alphabetically by town. The list provides a wide selection of hotels throughout Austria with a brief description, an illustration and pertinent information on each one.

For some of you, cost will not be a factor if the hotel is outstanding. For others, budget will guide your choices. The appeal of a simple little inn with rustic wooden furniture will beckon some, while the glamor of ornate ballrooms dressed with crystal chandeliers and gilt mirrors will appeal to others. What we have tried to do is to indicate what each hotel has to offer and to describe the setting, so that you can make the choice to suit your own preferences and holiday. We feel if you know what to expect, you will not be disappointed so we have tried to be candid and honest in our appraisals.

Austria has a wonderful palette of hotels - delightful lakeside manors, fabulous ski resorts, luxury city hotels, simple farmhouses, fascinating castles. A variety to satisfy the whim and pocketbook of every traveler.   Salzburg and Vienna are expensive, though certainly no more so than popular metropolitan areas anywhere in the world.   But once in the countryside, the choices are superb and the prices incredibly reasonable, especially in the small country inn or gasthaus.   Even though the tab is low, you will frequently find beautiful decor in the dining rooms and linen tablecloths, fresh flowers and candles on the tables.   Normally though, do not expect too much in the bedrooms - usually the antique ambiance is concentrated in the dining rooms,   though there are some outstanding exceptions which are noted under the various hotel descriptions.   Austria has her own special blend of hotels. A few main categories are as follows:

CASTLES: Whereas every little village seems to have an inn, every hilltop seems to have a castle.   Happily, many of these have been converted into hotels providing some of the best travel buys in Europe.   The majority of castle hotels have a faded elegance - those less polite might say a bit shabby.   But who could care that the guestrooms are not "decorator perfect" when the antique four-poster bed is fit for a king?   What does it matter if the Oriental carpet is frayed when the room comes alive with stories of another era when the the countess as a child danced around the Christmas tree?   Who can complain if the garden is no longer a spectacle of manicured perfection when photos create visions of a past when beautiful ladies dressed in satin sipped tea on the terrace?   There are some castles whose decor is impeccable and whose bathrooms sparkle with all the latest modern fixtures. Castles still owned by the original titled families are often the most interesting. Prices are often amazingly low and with your room comes a slice of romance and history.

FARMHOUSES: Many farmhouses have been turned into inns.   These are usually in the country near small towns.   Frequently the dining rooms exude a rustic charm with splendid paneling and sturdy little chairs whose backs are carved with hearts.   Bedrooms are clean simple with puffy down comforters on the beds.

HUNTING LODGES: Hunting was *the* sport for the landed gentry and it seems, in addition to his palace and castle, every nobleman had his own hunting lodge tucked away in the woods. Many of these are now wonderful hotels whose walls are adorned with trophies and a patchwork of photographs hinting at a way of life long gone. Hunting lodges are usually not deluxe. Most of them are quite like they used to be - rustic, simple rooms, lounges where men could sit and discuss the day's hunt, pleasant dining rooms serving an abundance of food (often featuring game, always featuring fresh fruits and vegetables from the garden), guestrooms clean and comfortable but not fancy.

PALACES: Most of the palaces are located in or near cities and were previously private estates of the nobility. Some are only reflections of the grandeur of the past and could do with a bit of sprucing up, but the price is usually very low, especially considering the romantic atmosphere. Other palaces are superbly maintained, fit for a king, and very expensive.

HOTEL RATES AND INFORMATION

In the back section of this guide there is a complete list of the recommended hotels with rates quoted in Austrian shillings (AUS).   We have strived to be as accurate as possible in giving prices in effect at the time of publication.   The rates shown (which include breakfast, taxes and service) are for two persons sharing a room.   It is impossible to cover completely every price possibility because most hotels have an intricate system of rates.   There are winter prices and summer prices and "in between season" prices.   There are rooms without private baths and luxury suites with two bathrooms.   There are special weekly bargains and holiday surcharges. There is not space to give you each and every price for each hotel.   However, we believe that you will be able to get a "ball park" figure of what to expect to pay by converting the Austrian shilling - your bank will be able to give you the current conversion rate.

HOTEL RESERVATIONS

People often ask, "Do I need a hotel reservation?" The answer really depends on how flexible you want to be, how tight your schedule is, which season you are traveling, and how disappointed you would be if your first choice is unavailable.

It is not unusual for the major tourist cities to be completely sold out during the peak season of June through September.   Hotel space in the cities is especially crowded, particularly during certain events such as the Music Festival in Salzburg each summer.   So unless you don't mind taking your chances on a last minute cancellation or staying on the outskirts of a town, make a reservation.   Space in the countryside is a little easier.   However, if you have your heart set on some special little inn, you certainly should reserve as soon as your travel dates are firm.

Reservations are confining.   Most hotels will want a deposit to hold your room and frequently refunds are difficult should you change your plans - especially at the last minute.   So it is a double bind.   Making reservations locks you into a solid frame-work, but without reservations you might be stuck with accommodations you do not like.

For those who like the security blanket of each night preplanned so that once you leave home you do not have to worry about where to rest your head each night, there are several options for making reservations which we have listed below.

TRAVEL AGENT: A travel agent can be of great assistance - particularly if your own time is valuable.   A knowledgeable agent can handle all of the details of your holiday and "tie" it all together for you in a neat little package including hotel reservations, airline tickets, boat tickets, train reservations, ferry schedules, opera tickets, etc.   For your airline tickets there will be no service fee, but travel agencies make a charge for their other services, such as hotel reservations, theater tickets, ferries and train reservations.   The best advice is to talk with your local agent.   Be frank about how much you want to spend and ask exactly what he can do for you and what the charges will be.   Although the travel agency in your town might not be familiar with all the little places in this guide, since many are so tiny that they appear in no other major sources, loan them your book - it is written as a guide for travel agents as well as for individual travelers.   (Note for travel agents who read this guide: most of the small inns in this guide pay no commission.)

LETTER: If you start early, you can write to the hotels directly for your reservations.   There are certainly many benefits to this in that you can be specific as to your exact preferences.   The important point is to be brief in your request. Clearly state the following: number of people in your party; how many rooms you desire; whether you want a private bathroom; date of arrival and date of departure; ask the rate per night and the deposit needed.   When you receive a reply send the deposit and ask for a receipt.   When corresponding with Austria be sure to spell out the month: do not use numbers since in Europe they reverse our system - e.g. 6/9 means September 6 to a European, not June 9.   Mail to Europe is sometimes slow so allow about a month for a reply.   Although most hotels can understand a letter written in English, on page 189 we have provided a reservation request letter written in German with an English translation.

TELEPHONE: One of the most satisfactory ways to make a reservation is to call long distance. The cost is minimal if you direct dial and you can have your answer immediately. If space is not available, you can then decide on an alternate. Ask your local operator about the best time to call for the lowest rates. Consider the time change and what time it is in Austria so that you can then call during their business day. Basically, the system is to dial 011, the international code, then 43, Austria's code. Compose these five numbers then dial the city code and the hotel telephone number which appear under the hotel listings. Before the city code there is a 0 - if you are dialing from outside Austria you omit it from the phone number.

TELEX: If you have access to a telex machine, this is another efficient way to reach a hotel. When a hotel has a telex, the number is included under the hotel listings. Again, be sure to be specific as to your arrival and departure dates, number in your party, and what type of room you want. And, of course, be sure to include your telex number for their response.

U.S. REPRESENTATIVE: Some hotels in Austria have a United States representative through whom reservations can be made. Many of these representatives have a toll free telephone number for your convenience. This is an extremely efficient way to secure a reservation. However, if you are on a strict budget you might find it less expensive to make the reservation yourself since sometimes a representative makes a charge for his service, only reserves the more expensive rooms, or quotes a higher price to protect himself against currency fluctuations and administrative costs. Futhermore, usually only the larger or more expensive hotels can afford the luxury of a representative in the United States - so many of the smaller inns must be contacted directly. Nevertheless, this is an excellent way to make a reservation, and United States representatives and their telephone numbers are included in the hotel section of this guide. If you plan carefully, by studying the hotel section you can chose hotels which have the same local representative and one telephone call can complete a bulk of your trip.

ITINERARIES

The first section of this guide outlines itineraries throughout Austria.   You should be able to find an itinerary, or section of an itinerary, to fit your exact time frame and suit your own particular interests.   You can custom tailor your own itinerary by combining segments of itineraries or using two "back to back".

The itineraries do not indicate a specific number of nights at each destination, since to do so seemed much too confining.   Again, personality dictates what is best for a particular situation.   Some travelers like to see as much as possible in a short period of time and do not mind rising with the birds each morning to begin a new adventure.   For others, just the thought of packing and unpacking each night makes them shudder in horror and they would never stop for less than three or four nights at any one destination.   A third type of tourist does not like to travel at all. The destination is the focus and he will use this guide to find the "perfect" resort from which he will never wander except for daytime excursions.   So use this guide as a reference from which to plan your very own personalized trip.   We cannot, however, help adding our recommendation: do not rush.   Learn to travel as the Europeans do.   Allow sufficient time to settle into a hotel properly and absorb the special ambiance each has to offer.   One hotel owner commented that the Americans travel so fast they do not always remember where they are, and told the story of stopping to see if she could assist an American woman studying her map in great frustration on a street corner in Vienna.   She asked if she could help - only to find the poor lady was looking for St. Mark's Square in Venice!

Please note that although a hotel is suggested for each destination in an itinerary, the hotel is just that - a SUGGESTION.   Perhaps the hotel seems over your budget, or too fancy, or too simple.   Or just not "you".   If this is the case, look in the back of the book and choose an alternative. To make your choice easier should you prefer another inn (or not be able to secure a reservation in your first choice of hotel), each itinerary map indicates by a small star other towns in the area where you can find recommended hotels.

MAPS

With each itinerary there is a map showing the routing and suggesting places of interest along the way. These are artist's renderings and are not intended to replace a good commercial map. To supplement our routings you will need a set of detailed maps which will indicate all of the highway numbers, expressways, alternative little roads, expressway access points, exact mileages, etc. Our suggestion would be to purchase a comprehensive selection of both city maps and regional maps before your departure, and with a highlight pen mark your own "personalized" itinerary and pinpoint your city hotels. (Note: frequently in Austria the hotels do not have a street address - especially in small towns the town itself is the only address. However, in most cases the tourist bureau does an excellent job of placing signs strategically to guide the tourist to each of the hotels once you are close.) Bookstores can usually order maps for you if they do not have them in stock. The Michelin maps are exceptionally good: one reason being that if you want to deviate from an itinerary to explore on your own, Michelin marks in green the most scenic or interesting roads. Michelin maps also tie in with their excellent "Green Guides" which are an outstanding reference for details on when museums are open, etc.

MUSIC

Many of the world's greatest musical geniuses were born within a few miles of Vienna. Incredibly, they were all born within a relatively short span of history and their lives and music were interrelated. Haydn, Mozart, Liszt, Strauss, Schubert, Bruckner - just a few of the men whose musical compositions have added so much joy to the world. No one knows for sure what caused this sublime surge of talent. Many experts think it was probably due to the Austrians' innate love of music and to the fact that it was the style for the wealthy nobility to "sponsor" musical genius - in much the same way that the Italian aristocracy sponsored artists. Whatever the reason, the world is much richer thanks to these sons of Austria. Reading their biographies and listening to their music will greatly add to the enjoyment of your holiday.

PROVINCES

Austria is divided into nine regions, or provinces, two of which are very small areas that encircle the cities of Salzburg and Vienna. Some of the provinces have two completely different spellings - one the English version and one the Austrian version. On the small map below both are given so that you can recognize either.

Provinces of Austria

SHOPPING

Most shops are open from 9:00 AM to 6:00 PM and closed for an hour or two in the middle of the day when the shopkeeper goes home for lunch. In resort areas, some of the shops are open seven days a week, but in most towns the stores are closed Saturday afternoons and Sunday. The shops are filled with many tantalizing items attractively and artfully displayed. Some of the favorite items to take home are:

CERAMICS: Ceramics are made in Gmunden, which is in the lake district near Salzburg. You can buy anything from a entire dinner set to a beer mug. If your itinerary does not take you to Gmunden, the ceramics are also available in shops in Salzburg, Vienna and Innsbruck.

DIRNDLS: Dirndls are charming pinafores usually of provincial print material worn with a white blouse and apron. All sizes are available from adorable tiny dresses for little girls to matching costumes for mommy and grandmother. In addition to all sizes, the dresses come in all fabrics and designs from gay daytime cotton models to fabulous pure silk high-fashion designer creations.

GLASSWARE: In the medieval town of Rattenburg, along the Inn River near Innsbruck, you can buy from a wonderful selection of glasses of all kinds. These are made by local craftsmen who came from Czechoslovakia as refugees and brought their craft with them. You can have your glassware engraved while you wait or have it mailed home.

LEDERHOSEN: A trip to Austria would not be complete without bringing home a pair of the wonderful leather shorts for all the men and little boys in the family. They are not expensive and just do not wear out.

Getreidegasse
Salzburg's Main Shopping Street

Introduction

HATS: It is fun to bring home a jaunty Austrian felt hat.

LEATHER GOODS: The leather in Austria is especially beautiful: not only is it soft and lovely, but also skillfully styled. The skirts and jackets are expensive, but absolutely gorgeous.

PETITPOINT: Vienna is famous for its beautiful petitpoint needlework which is available in handbags, eyeglass cases, belts, etc. There are many cheap imitations in the souvenir shops, but the real thing is very expensive and very exquisite.

SKI EQUIPMENT: The ski equipment in Austria does not seem any great buy; however, it is fun to bring home a pair of skis or boots, if for no other reason than the memory - especially if you were on a ski holiday.

SWEATERS: There are many beautiful woolen sweaters for men, women and children. Especially comfortable, and typically Austrian, are the sweaters which look like jackets.

TEXTILES: Austria has lovely materials. The "country motif" designs are popular and make beautiful curtains, tablecloths, napkins, etc.

WOODEN BOXES: Wooden boxes of all sizes and styles, painted with gay Tyrolean designs of flowers and hearts, are available.

If you are planning to do much shopping, you should also plan to take advantage of the tax credit. Austria has a 20% tax which is refundable if you buy over 1,000 shillings' worth of goods. At most tourist oriented shops, you ask for a tax refund form which the store will fill out. In the cities this is a common request, but in the hinterlands they will not know what you are talking about. As you leave the country you MUST have this form stamped by the Austrian tax inspector. There are inspectors at the airport and the border crossings. If you are leaving by train, you must get off the train at the border and have the inspector at the customs office stamp the form. Keep your purchases together because the customs agent will probably want to see what you have bought. If you are returning into Austria you can go back to the store and they will reimburse the tax you paid. If you are leaving the country, you can often receive a refund at the departure point. Most of the stores give you an information sheet that explains all the different places you can receive tax refunds.

TRANSPORTATION

BOATS

Most of the lakes have ferryboats which operate from Spring to Fall, and there is no lovelier way to explore Austria's lakes than from the deck of a boat. No reservations are needed and the schedule is always posted at the pier. Be sure to be on time because the boats glide in and out of the docks like clockwork and passengers that are late are left behind.

A popular boat excursion is the ferryboat which plies the Danube between Passau and Vienna. If you wish to just take a segment between two towns you need no reservation; simply buy your ticket and climb aboard. However, if you are taking the entire trip and desire a cabin, then reservations are needed in advance. These ferries are not deluxe, but lots of fun and a marvelous way to see the countryside.

Another option is to take the hydrofoil which links Vienna with Budapest. The trip to Budapest takes four and a half hours while the return trip takes five and a half. Reservations should be made in advance.

TRAINS

Austria has excellent trains and a spiderweb of routes which link most of the cities and small towns. In addition to the excellent system and dependable time schedules, for the train buffs there is another wonderful bonus - marvelous narrow gauge trains which chug behind their puffing black steam engines into some of the most beautiful and remote areas of Austria. Originally these were built by the emperor so that he could keep in contact with people living in isolated mountain regions. Later, after roads were built, many of the trains remained - a reminder of a romantic past. These trains look too cute to be real. As you are driving along, you will hear a "toot toot" and winding through the valley will be a gay little engine pulling a stream of brightly painted cars, loaded with passengers. On some of these trains, you can even be the conductor and command the train from a perch in the engine, although your conductor's status must usually be reserved in advance. Contact the Austrian Tourist Office (500 Fifth Avenue, New York, NY 10110, tel: (212) 944-6880) for further information concerning when and where the "Toy Trains" operate.

In each train station there is usually a desk where someone speaks English to assist you with schedules. There is also an excellent guide you can buy at the train station called "Fahrplane" which has a map and all the schedules for trains, boats and buses.

On international trains which whip between European countries you usually need a reservation and sometimes must pay a supplement for a special deluxe express train. However, for the local trains you rarely need a seat reservation - if you have a ticket, you can normally hop aboard and find a seat. The cars are marked on the outside first or second class and within both categories are designated seating areas for smoking and non smoking. Some of the trains have dining cars, some have a man who walks through selling snacks, and some have no food service.

For the trains within Austria you can buy individual tickets, use your Eurailpass or buy an Austrian Rail Pass (which cannot be purchased until you arrive in Europe). The Austrian Rail Passes are issued in either first or second class for nine days, sixteen days or one month.

UMLAUTS

I would like to clarify the approach in this text to the use of umlauts. An umlaut is a grammatical punctuation that appears as two dots above a vowel changing the sound of the vowel. An "e" immediately following the identified vowel will achieve the same result. Our printing facilities do not include the umlaut punctuation symbol and yet we were concerned as to whether or not to add the "e" to achieve the proper Germanic spelling of a word. As most Americans would not realize the significance of the umlaut and read the addition of the "e" as a spelling change, we decided it best to ignore the umlaut altogether in the hopes of simplifying the text, avoiding a confusion on the part of the reader, trusting that those with a working knowledge of the German language will forgive our grammatical omission and understand.

WEATHER

Austria's weather is fickle. There is rain. Lots of rain. It can be pouring in the morning, and be a beautiful sunny day by noon. Do not count on warm days. Consider yourself lucky if it is balmy and be prepared for chilly weather with woolly sweaters which can be pulled off as the day warms. You may be lucky and have your entire holiday a collection of perfect days, but as you admire the incredibly green fields and splendid array of flowers, your common sense will tell you that this lush splendor is not the result of a man-made irrigation system. Be prepared with the proper clothing and enjoy Austria rain or shine, snow or sun, cold or warm.

WHAT TO WEAR

For winter bring warm coats, sweaters, gloves, snug hats, and boots. The rest of the year a layered effect will equip you for any kind of weather: skirts or trousers combined with blouses or shirts which can then be "built upon" in layers of sweaters depending upon the chill of the day. A raincoat is a must, along with a folding umbrella. Sturdy, comfortable walking shoes are recommended not only for roaming the many beckoning mountain trails, but also for negotiating cobbled streets. Daytime dress is casual, but in the evening it is appropriate to dress for dinner. Nothing elaborate is necessary, but a sport coat and tie for men and a dress or sweater and skirt for women. It is a courtesy to the hotels to change into more formal attire in the evenings when dining in their restaurants.

WINES

Although not as famous as those of France, Germany and Italy, the Austrian wines are delicious and plentiful. The majority of grapes are grown in Lower Austria, but vineyards are also found in the provinces of Burgenland, Vienna and Styria. Wine labels usually indicate the region of their origin and the grape variety. There is no single "wine road" in Austria, but a series of short excursions in various areas will be rewarding for the wine enthusiast. In lower Austria the Wachau provides a delightful 30-mile stretch of terraced vineyards which line the steep banks of the Danube as it winds its way between Melk and Krems. Another lovely route is found near the Hungarian border, where fabulous wines are grown around the charming old town of Rust. Another popular "wine route" is in the rolling hills around Vienna.

The Heurigen are simple homes or little shops whose proprietors offer for sale the wines from the previous year's harvest. A branch of greenery is hung over the door to announce to all that wine sampling is available inside. Often tables are set outside on a vine-covered terrace where light snacks are also served. To complete the enjoyment, there is often music and singing. There are many popular Heurigen near Vienna, but many of these have become a bit trite with the arrival of busloads of tourists. Most fun are the "real" Heurigen in the countryside - frequently in the home of a vintner who opens his doors to the public and serves his latest wines accompanied by simple food. The Heuriger is not a new idea: it traces back to the 18th century when Joseph II ruled that individual vintners could sell their own wines privately.

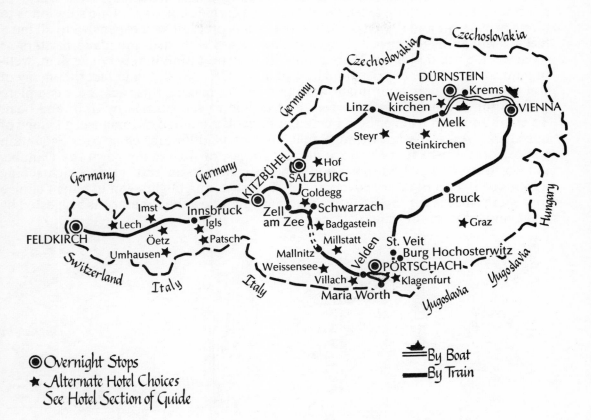

Highlights of Austria by Train & Boat

DÜRNSTEIN
Krems
Weissen-kirchen
Linz
Melk
VIENNA
Steyr
Steinkirchen
Hof
KITZBÜHEL
SALZBURG
Goldegg
Bruck
Germany
Germany
Germany
Imst
Innsbruck
Schwarzach
Lech
Igls
Zell am See
Badgastein
Graz
FELDKIRCH
Öetz
Patsch
Millstatt
St. Veit
Umhausen
Mallnitz
Velden
Burg Hochosterwitz
Weissensee
PÖRTSCHACH
Switzerland
Italy
Villach
Klagenfurt
Italy
Maria Worth
Czechoslovakia
Czechoslovakia
Czechoslovakia
Hungary
Yugoslavia
Yugoslavia
Yugoslavia

◉ Overnight Stops
★ Alternate Hotel Choices
See Hotel Section of Guide

⛴ By Boat
▬ By Train

29

Highlights of Austria by Train and Boat

Many travelers long for the freedom to travel at their own pace, to choose their own hotels, to avoid the confinement of a packaged bus tour, but their sense of adventure does not quite extend to driving in a foreign country.   One solution is to hire a private car and driver; however, the cost is prohibitively expensive to all but a lucky few who never have to concern themselves with such mundane matters as money.   Do not despair.   Austria's public transportation is very convenient, well-organized, moderate in price, and best of all - FUN.   Such fun in fact that many of you who usually rent a car might want to consider making this vacation a complete holiday for all, including the driver, and decide to see Austria by train and boat. To climb aboard a train or boat immediately evokes a mood of romance, a twinge of nostalgia.   As you whiz through meadows of wildflowers, chug over mountain passes, zip through tunnels, trace narrow gorges, or float lazily down the Danube, the world is yours.   Transportation is not a means to an end.   It is a sightseeing adventure.   This itinerary covers some of Austria's highlights - an excellent choice for seeing Austria for the first time whether you follow the itinerary as suggested by train and boat or in your own car.

Durnstein

Should you choose to travel by train and boat, you really must travel lightly.   To lug a heavy suitcase from train to taxi to hotel soon dims the joy and the journey becomes drudgery.   But if each person has just one small suitcase which can easily be swung up onto the train and again onto the rack in the compartment, freedom and adventure are yours.

Once you decide upon an exact routing for your trip, you can compare the cost of buying individual tickets from town to town versus an Austrian Rail Pass (or using a Eurailpass if Austria is being combined with travel to other countries in Europe). The Austrian Rail Pass cannot be purchased until you arrive in Europe, but can be bought at all Austrian railroad stations and at the ticket offices of the central rail stations in Frankfurt, Munich or Zurich.   Rail passes can be purchased in either first class or second class for nine days, sixteen days or one month.   When purchasing your rail pass advise the agent the class of service, the duration of the pass and what day you want to begin using it.   He will issue you a small card and from that time on, all you need to do is hop onto the train and show the card to the conductor as he comes through. The Austrian Rail Pass also gives a fifty per cent discount on the Danube Cruises.   Below are a few helpful words to know when traveling by public transportation:

BAHNHOF: Train station
SCHIFFAHRT: Boat dock
STANDSEILBAHN: Cable car
KABINENSEILBAHN: Gondola
ABFAHRT: Time of departure
NACH: Travelling to
BAHNSTEIG: Platform number at the train station
GLEIS: Track number

With these few terms you should be in business.

IMPORTANT NOTE: Times are given within this itinerary as a reference so that you can see how the pieces of the itinerary fit together and the approximate time to allow between destinations. Since schedules constantly change, especially between seasons, please verify each of the times. When you purchase your tickets, buy a book called Fahrplane, which costs about $4.00 and gives the schedules for all the boats, trains, cable cars and buses in Austria. Published seasonally, it is a wealth of information. In the front of the book instructions are given for understanding the guide and with a little study you should be an expert. (If you have doubts about your ability, read the guide and check the times with the information desk at the train station to be sure you are correct. Almost every station has an information desk where an English speaking agent can assist you with train schedules.)

ORIGINATING CITY   SALZBURG

Salzburg is magic. A very special city with the ambiance of a small town; a fairy-tale town of narrow streets, colorful old houses, charming little squares, enticing shops, whimsical wrought-iron signs, men wearing leather breeches, women in colorful dirndls. An enormous grey castle guards the city from the hilltop, a beautiful river runs through the center and superb mountains rise just a glance away. The old town is so picturesque that before you do any major sightseeing you will certainly just want to meander through the maze of streets which frequently converge like spokes into small squares. It is easy to get lost, but the town is so small that you can quickly find a familiar landmark and be on your way again.

When you settle down to sightseeing, you will be pleased to realize that most places of interest are within easy walking distance. You will want to pay a visit to the intriguing fortress, Hohensalzburg, which looms above the city and is reached by funicular from the edge of town, St. Peter's Abbey founded in 696, the Cathedral with its three massive bronze doors, the Glockenspiel whose bells play daily at 7:00 AM, 11:00 AM and 6:00 PM, the Residenze which was the seat of the powerful Prince-Archbishops of Salzburg, the Residenze Gallery with its wealth of 16th- to 19th-century paintings, and Mozart's birthplace.

Just across the river from the heart of Old Salzburg - an easy walk over the pedestrian bridge - are the Mirabell Gardens which you should not miss. The Schloss Mirabell and the gardens were built in 1606 by the Archbishop Wolf Dietrich for his mistress, Salome Alt. As you walk through lovely terraced lawns you can imagine the Archbishop strolling with his "favorite" while their children romped nearby.

Before arriving in Salzburg check with the Austrian National Tourist Office to see what special events are happening during your visit. A popular event in late summer is the Salzburg Music Festival. Should your visit coincide with this, you will need to plan far in advance, not only for tickets, but also for hotel space. One event you should include is the Marionette Opera, located just across the river near the Mirabell Gardens. The marrionettes usually perform Mozart's operas. The exquisite scenery, splendid marrionettes dressed in intricate costumes, and the agility and talent of the skillful fingers manipulating the strings combine to make a magical evening you will not forget. Arrive early so that you can spend time studying the showcases of marrionettes from past performances. Their tiny costumes of fine silks, handmade laces, velvets, and feathers are amazing.

There are many excellent day trips available from Salzburg. One of the tours takes in the beautiful lakes and towering Dachstein mountains - this area is called the Salzkammergut. Other tours go to the salt mines - the name of Salzburg evolves from "salz" or "salt" and "burg" or "fortress". The mining of salt was responsible for the wealth and power of Salzburg and the mines can still be visited, making an exciting tour. There are also ice caves near Salzburg - a beautiful outing not only because the caves are fascinating with their fabulous formations of ice, but the scenery is so lovely too.

Salzburg has a selection of hotels in all price ranges. Some are in the heart of Salzburg, others in the suburbs within easy driving distance (or in some cases convenient to public transportation.) The hotel section describes the various recommendations.

DESTINATION I   DURNSTEIN   Schloss Durnstein

It is a short cab ride from the center of the Old Quarter to the train station. On rainy days it sometimes takes ten or fifteen minutes to summon a cab so allow plenty of time. Your train journey takes you from SALZBURG to MELK, a boat station for the Danube ferry. There is a marvelous Benedictine abbey at Melk which dominates the hill above the town and overlooks the river. Those who want to visit the abbey should leave Salzburg about 8:40 AM, change trains in LINZ, and arrive in Melk in time to take a tour of the abbey. However, the direct train is easier so this is suggested:

9:57 AM Leave Salzburg by train
1:41 PM Arrive Melk

After leaving Salzburg it is only minutes until you are out of the city and surrounded by the beautiful hills and lakes which make the area around Salzburg so famous. The landscape is lovely, with high mountains in the distance and rolling low hills dotted with farms in the foreground. As the train nears Linz, industrial areas begin to appear, but once out of the city the scenery is again one of pastoral beauty. As you near Melk watch closely, for you will have a beautiful view of the Melk Abbey.

When you arrive in Melk, a five-minute taxi ride takes you to the ferry stop.   There are two docks, one for the large ferry which goes between PASSAU and VIENNA and another for the local ferry.   If the taxi driver does not speak English, you might want to jot down on a slip of paper "SCHIFFAHRT - WIEN".   This will tell him that you want the boat dock for the ferry going to Vienna.

Buy your ticket at the boat dock.   Purchase a ticket to Vienna, which will allow you a free stopover at tonight's destination DURNSTEIN.   Once you have your ticket, I suggest that you check your bags so you will be free to walk around until the boat arrives.   There is a baggage room at the ticket office - if it is closed I am sure the person who sells the tickets will open it for you.   A nice restaurant, the JENSCH MELKER FAHRHAUS, is just a two-minute walk from the dock: its beautiful riverfront terrace is a great place to relax while waiting for the ferry.

As the time for the ferry to arrive draws near, people suddenly congregate.   The recently deserted dock teams with activity: young boys with bicycles, families with picnic baskets, hikers in sturdy shoes with knapsacks on their shoulders, busloads of tourists.   Once on board, "stake your claim" and find a table and some chairs where you can enjoy the journey.   The ferry has a dining room and several snack bars.   If you want complete freedom to roam the boat unencumbered, ask the agent, in the little office to the left as you board, to put your suitcases in the luggage room - this costs about a dollar per item.

2:00 PM Leave Melk by Danube ferry
3:45 PM Arrive Durnstein

The section of the Danube between Melk and Durnstein is very famous and very beautiful.   During these few miles, the river lazily loops and turns as it cuts its way through the hills which sometimes rise so precipitously as to give a fjord-like beauty.   This is the famous WACHAU area of Austria which produces some of Austria's finest wines.   Along the banks of the river, vineyards terrace up the steep hillsides, small wine-producing villages nestle at every hospitable strand of shore and romantic ruins of castles decorate the skyline. En route the major points of interest are pointed out in English.

Your destination is the enchanting village of Durnstein. This tiny hamlet, perched on a ledge overlooking the Danube, is fairytale perfect. Still walled, the village boasts colorful houses, a tiny square, a lovely monastery with an especially attractive courtyard, and the ruins of a castle atop the hill. The castle has its own "fairytale" story. In 1192 Leopold V captured England's King Richard the Lionheart and hid him in Durnstein Castle. No one knew where the king was imprisoned. Blondel, the King's minstrel, devised a plan to find his master. He drifted from castle to castle playing King Richard's favorite songs. When Blondel reached Durnstein, as he played and sang beneath the castle walls, Richard heard and joined in the singing. Naturally, he was rescued and the story had a happy ending. Durnstein has a fabulous hotel, built into the cliffs high above the Danube, the SCHLOSS DURNSTEIN. Advise the hotel what time you will be arriving on the ferry and they will have a porter waiting at the pier. He will carry your suitcases and guide you up the tunnel which cuts through the rocks and opens like magic on the upper level into a beautiful garden. A terrace with tables and chairs set among the trees and flowers wraps around the side of the hotel. Here in fair weather you dine with a glorious view of the river as it winds its way toward Vienna. On the opposite bank is another small village and in the distance hills rise to form a backdrop to the idyllic scene. The interior is superb and you live like royalty. Ornate antiques are lavishly used in the reception hall, small lounges and bar. The bedrooms all vary, but most of them also have antiques. The beautiful dining room serves gourmet food,the specialties being fresh fish and veal. If it is the berry season you will love their raspberry souffle.

Durnstein is so small it only takes a short walk to explore from one gate to the other. Nevertheless, the Schloss Durnstein is such a splendid hotel, the food so delicious, the setting so spectacular, and the town of Durnstein so romantic that it would make a wonderful stopover for a few days. There are many paths to explore, including a walk to the Weissenkirchen, another beautiful old wine village located a little over 2 miles away. With careful planning you can hike and return to WEISSENKIRCHEN by ferry to Durnstein. If you prefer to exercise by sitting on plump cushions in the sun, you can do so beside a heated pool within an enclosed garden - a delightful oasis.

Schloss Durnstein
Durnstein

DESTINATION II   VIENNA   Hotel im Palais Schwarzenberg

When you must leave Durnstein, the porter will carry your bags to the pier. It is possible to take a train from Durnstein to Vienna, but the ferry is more fun. Checkout time from the hotel is noon, but you can leave your suitcases at the front desk and have one last lingering meal before leaving.

3:55 PM Leave Durnstein by ferry
8:00 PM Arrive Vienna

The first town you come to is KREMS. As you near the town watch for the magnificent Benedictine monastery, GOTTWEIG ABBEY, which dominates the top of a hill. Although it is far in the distance on the right bank of the river, it appears quite dramatic and beautiful in the late afternoon sunlight due to its immense size. After Krems, the banks of the river flatten out and become less scenic, but before you have time to become restless, you arrive at an enormous lock which drops the boat from the high level of a dam to the lower flow of the river below. It is fascinating to watch the boat sink about 40 feet and, as the gates slowly swing open, glide out into the river below. Beyond the lock you will see on the right a large nuclear power station which, although finished for several years, has never been put into operation. There is a second lock to navigate before you see the distant skyline of VIENNA.

Since the ferry does not arrive in Vienna until evening, it is wise to have dinner before the boat docks. The ferry's dining room has large windows so you do not miss any of the action as you enjoy your meal.

Upon arrival in Vienna, take a cab to the HOTEL IM PALAIS SCHWARZEN-BERG. Although an expensive, luxury category hotel, it is so special that it is an irresistible suggestion for your home in Vienna. If the price is above your budget, look in the hotel section in the back of this guide for alternatives. The Palais Schwarzenberg is far more than a hotel, it is a fabulous palace built in the early part of the 18th century. In 1940 it was confiscated by the Gestapo, then later damaged in the Allied bombing of Vienna, but today it is back in the hands of Prince Schwarzenberg. The family has their home in one wing and the hotel in another. The core of the original palace is used for concerts, fancy receptions and formal dinners in honor of visiting dignitaries. In the gravel walkway there is an asphalt underbase for helicopters which frequently whirl in to deposit high-powered diplomats and entrepreneurs from around the world. The Palace is gorgeous. In the original palace there are frescoes by the famous artist Daniel Gran, paintings by Werner Tamm, Chinese lacquer from the 17th century period of the emperor K'ang-hsi, and even two fabulous large paintings by Rubens. A manicured garden, with fountains, statues, velvet green lawns and pathways circling beneath enormous trees stretches for over 18 acres behind the building.

The hotel's intimate small reception room, secluded writing room, cozy bar, flower filled tea room, gorgeous dining room and glass-enclosed garden terrace are exquisite. You definitely have the feeling of being in a private home. And, in case you don't know any kings, this might be your only chance to be entertained like royalty. The 42 bedrooms are beautifully furnished: the less expensive ones are large and lovely but look out over the central courtyard used for parking; the most expensive rooms and suites are in the original palace and have garden views. With so few rooms it is impossible to guarantee a garden view during the high season. The Palais Schwarzenberg is within two blocks of the famous ring which encircles the heart of old Vienna and in less than fifteen minutes you can easily walk to most points of interest.

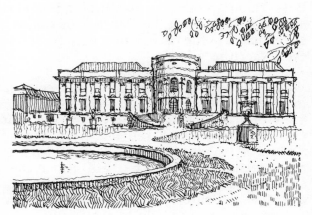

Hotel im Palais Schwarzenberg
Vienna

There is so much to see and do in Vienna that it almost demands a book in itself. Buy a city map and a sightseeing guide. If you enjoy walking, there is an excellent book by J. Sydney Jones called "Vienna Inside-Out" which gives sixteen walking tours of the city. To get acquainted with the major points of interest you will probably want to take a city tour and then go back to savor at length your favorite museums, cathedrals and palaces. There are many tour operators and your hotel will have their brochures. However, if there are several persons in your party, check the price of a private car with English speaking guide. You can cover so much more of the city and squeeze so much more information into a small amount of time when you do not have to wait for a busload of other passengers and a private car does not cost much more if you share the expense. You will certainly want to see the Opera House, Hofburg Palace, St. Stephen's Cathedral, Belvedere Palace, the Burgtheater, the Lipizzaner horses at the Spanish Riding School, and of course the beautiful Schonbrunn Palace and Gardens. In summer the Opera, the Boys' Choir and the Spanish Riding School close, but there is always plenty to see and do. Even when the Opera is on holiday, the city is filled with music. There are concerts in the parks and special performances in some of the palaces - music is everywhere in Vienna.

When you begin to plan your holiday, contact the Austrian National Tourist Office in New York (telephone: 212-944-6880) to find what will be highlighted while you are visiting. Tickets for the Opera, the Spanish Riding School and Vienna Boys' Choir must be purchased far in advance. The American tour company, Dial Austria (telephone: 800-221-4980), which is a representative for some hotels in the hotel section of this book, will also make reservations for special events. In addition to the endless variety of castles, museums, palaces, gardens, parks, churches and entertainment to be savored within Vienna, on the outskirts of the city you can enjoy a trip to the beautiful Vienna Woods, or a trip to Mayerling where the tragic Prince Rudolph, only son of the Emperor Franz Joseph, committed suicide with his young mistress, Baronesse Vetsera, in 1889. Or travel to Grinzing, to sample the new wines and join in with the music and gaiety. There is so much to see and do in Vienna that you could spend your entire holiday here.

After a busy sightseeing schedule, it will be a pleasant contrast to spend a few days in the south beside one of Austria's loveliest lakes, the WORTHERSEE.   The train connections are easy and the ride is especially beautiful.   You depart from the South Station, about a five-minute taxi ride from the Palais Schwarzenberg.

9:00 AM Leave Vienna South Station by train
1:30 PM Arrive Portschach am Worthersee

Leaving Vienna, the land is flat as you pass through small suburbs and commercial areas, but within an hour the panorama from your window is marvelous - beautiful wooded hills, lush green meadows, castles dotting mountaintops, rocky cliffs, small villages and tiny chapels.   You will not want to take your eyes from the window for fear of missing a magnificent castle partially hidden behind giant trees or an exquisite onion-domed little chapel on a mountain ledge.   In a couple of hours the train will arrive in BRUCK AN DER MUR which is a small industrial town at the junction of the Murz and Mur rivers. The train follows the Mur River west from Bruck.   For a short while the scene is industrial but soon the suburbs are behind you and you enter a serene rural area - a wide valley filled with fields of wheat and enclosed by forested hills.   Cows graze in square patches of meadow amongst the trees on the rolling hills.   About an hour from Bruck the train makes a curve to the south and heads for the large city of KLAGENFURT.   Watch closely because about fifteen minutes before the train comes to Klagenfurt, near the town of ST. VEIT AN DER GLAN, you will see on the left side of the train BURG HOCHOSTERWITZ, a fascinating castle dominating the top of a miniature mountain.   After leaving Klagenfurt, the train follows the lake and in a few minutes you are in PORTSCHACH.

When you arrive in Portschach take a cab to your hotel, SCHLOSS SEEFELS. This is anything but a simple hotel. This is a sophisticated, luxury resort. Relax and be pampered for a few days while you enjoy the beauty of Austria's warmest lake. This splendid lakefront mansion curves around a lush lawn which stretches down to the lake where a large square dock floats over the water for sunning and swimming. In addition, there is a swimming pool which cleverly meanders from the inside to outside so that swimmers can enjoy their sport in any kind of weather. Excellent tennis courts are located in front, there is golf available just a quick motor boat ride across the lake, ping pong, water skiing, sail-surfing, fishing - most anything can be arranged. Inside, the hotel is tastefully furnished with many antiques. The bedrooms are lovely with decorator-perfect coordinated draperies, chairs and bedspreads. Most of the rooms have views of the lake and many have balconies. The dining room is elegant, a wall of glass doors opening onto a large lakeview balcony.

Schloss Seefels
Worthersee-Portschach

The hotel is so peaceful you might not want to leave the premises, but if you do, there are many excursions available. Portschach is a small, touristy town, without much charm, but there are many points of interest nearby. You can ask the hotel concierge to arrange a tour. There is also a travel agency in the town of Portschach offering many packaged tours. Try at least to include a tour to Burg Hochosterwitz, the castle you saw earlier from the train. Be sure to wear sturdy shoes because you must walk up to the castle. Built on what looks like a toy mountain, the path zigzags up the hill crossing fortified bridges, little moats, drawbridges and, most fascinating of all, through FOURTEEN gates, each with its unique way to "do in" the enemy. Some gates have walls with spiked doors which descend from the ceiling, others have holes for hot oil, others inner rooms to capture the invader. It is lots of fun. As you near the summit there is a path leading off to an exquisite little chapel. Be sure to take the detour because the chapel is as pretty inside as it is out. Once you have conquered your castle, there is nothing of special interest - a small museum of arms, a few pictures and a very nice courtyard - the fun is in the approach. There is a nice restaurant in the courtyard for lunch or a glass of wine.

Another excursion is provided by the ferryboat around the lake, the complete circle taking several hours. It is fun to get off in one of the villages en route, do a little exploring, then board another ferry to continue your journey. The most attractive of the towns is MARIA WORTH, on a peninsula which juts into the lake across from the Schloss Seefels. A beautiful Gothic parish church is on the crest of the hill in the center of the village and makes a splendid picture as the boat draws near.

DESTINATION IV   KITZBUHEL   Romantic Hotel Tennerhof

There are many trains which pass through the Portschach station - watch for the one which will be marked to Salzburg. After boarding, settle back and relax: the scenery en route is sensational. The train follows the shoreline and then stops in the city of Villach before heading north.

```
 9:36 AM   Leave Portschach by train
12:02 PM   Arrive Schwarzach

12:16 PM   Leave Schwarzach by train
 1:41 PM   Arrive Kitzbuhel
```

SCHWARZACH is a small station and the connection is easy. The train to KITZBUHEL usually comes on the track adjacent to the one where you arrive and will be marked to INNSBRUCK. Do not be concerned when you board the train and it seems you are heading back the way you just came. You are. But in only a short while the train changes directions and heads directly west toward Kitzbuhel. The ride is lovely as the train follows a gentle valley bordered by low, tree-covered mountains. Before long you will see the lake, ZELL AM ZEE. The train traces its shoreline before rushing on again through the wide valley. Soon the soft hills swell into enormous rocky summits of great beauty which herald the arrival of Kitzbuhel.

Upon arrival in Kitzbuhel, take a five-minute cab ride to the ROMANTIK HOTEL TENNERHOF. The hotel, once an old chalet and now a deluxe inn, is on a gentle hillside, a fifteen-minute walk from the center of town. From the moment you step through the doors you will be enchanted, lovely antiques are everywhere and an elegant yet rustic decor appears throughout. There are three dining rooms, all beautiful and serving excellent, garden-fresh food. The bedrooms all vary, though they all have a rustic, friendly feeling. Many have genuine antique beds; some have balconies with views of the mountains. The coziest bedrooms are those in the original section of the chalet.

A short walk down the hill takes you to the gates of Kitzbuhel, a very popular tourist center both in summer and winter. Kitzbuhel is the epitome of what one expects when one thinks of the Tyrol - a colorful village whose painted buildings echo the past, charming little squares, inviting shops, walls surrounding the town, picturesque old gates, and mountains looming up from every view. Although this is a small town, there are a few sights to see such as the Pfarrkirche and the Liebfrauenkirche (two churches), both with lovely paintings to admire. But sightseeing is not the emphasis in Kitzbuhel - instead just relax and soak in the charm of the Tyrol. Try to stay several days, make shopping expeditions into town, sit by the pool in the garden at the hotel, take the cable car up to the mountain peaks and meander for miles along well marked paths through some of the loveliest scenery in Austria.

Romantik Hotel Tennerhof
Kitzbuhel

DESTINATION V   FELDKIRCH   Hotel Alpenrose

Note: Although this itinerary follows a route leading directly west to the scenic town of FELDKIRCH located almost on the Swiss border, there are several excellent options for those who either wish to travel on to Germany or else to complete their circle and return to Salzburg. As an example, there is a train which leaves Kitzbuhel about 9:00 AM and arrives in Munich about ll:40 AM. Or, for those returning to Salzburg, there is a train which leaves Kitzbuhel about 12:13 PM and arrives in Salzburg about 2:32 PM.

However, if you are heading into Switzerland, or have the time to extend your Austrian holiday, enjoy the beautiful train ride from Kitzbuhel to Feldkirch. The train should have a dining car if you wish to enjoy a meal en route.

12:40 PM Leave Kitzbuhel by train
 4:23 PM Arrive Feldkirch

As the train leaves Kitzbuhel the scenery is dazzling. Gigantic mountains soar into the sky - their jagged peaks scratching the clouds. The sullen grandeur of the mountains is intensified by the softness of the meadows in the foreground. It is so beautiful that you will be thankful you are on a train with no driving distractions. About an hour after leaving Kitzbuhel you arrive in INNSBRUCK. If you wish to do some sightseeing, either check your suitcases through to Feldkirch or deposit them in the baggage room at the Innsbruck train station.

As the train approaches, Innsbruck looks quite dismal, but within a few minutes of the station there is a colorful old city hiding behind ancient medieval walls. The shopping is mostly souvenir-tacky items, but there are many stunning old buildings, splendid churches, and a majestic central pedestrian square. If you want to see Innsbruck, get off the train, do your sightseeing, have lunch in one of the colorful outdoor restaurants and then take one of the later trains to Feldkirch.

When you arrive in Feldkirch, your hotel is located only minutes by cab from the train station. The HOTEL ALPENROSE, whose history dates back to 1550, is a simple yet outstanding little inn with only sixteen bedrooms. The owner, Rosi Gutwinski, speaks excellent English and welcomes you with an inborn graciousness. You will definitely feel that you are in a home rather than a hotel. Mrs Gutwinski's grandmother originally owned the hotel and many of her antiques accentuate the charm of both the reception and the bedrooms. The price is incredibly low for an inn of this quality in the center of a city. Only breakfast is served, but the hotel is located on a quiet little square only steps from the center of town with a wide choice of places to dine.

Hotel Alpenrose
Feldkirch

Feldkirch has not yet become "touristy". It is tiny, but reminiscent of Salzburg with its beautiful setting, maze of streets, and colorful old buildings. The mountains rise at the edge of town and, if you look up, you see a large castle commanding a rocky perch. Feldkirch still retains some of its old walls, old gates and towers. The two main streets are lined with picturesque arcaded houses with oriel windows, turrets and towers. Pretty shops stretch up and down the network of pedestrian streets, and outdoor cafes offer refreshments. This 13th-century town is truly a gem.

From Feldkirch you can conveniently take the train into Switzerland or Germany or make a circle back to Salzburg.

Hallstatt

Spectacular Lakes
& Mountains
of Salzkammergut

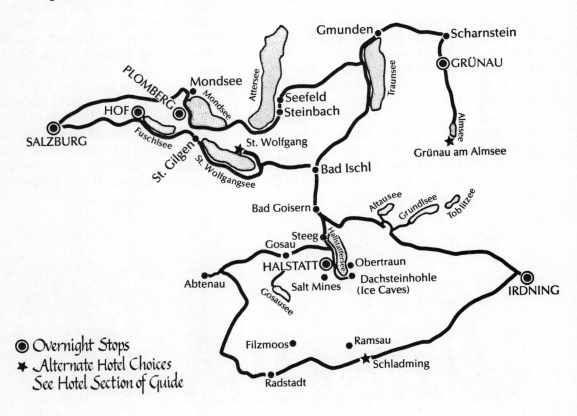

Spectacular Lakes and Mountains of Salzkammergut

The area close to Salzburg is called Salzkammergut, meaning "Land of the Salt Mines", a rather dreary title for one of the most beautiful sections of Austria. Salt, a precious commodity, was responsible for Salzburg's prominence and wealth, a wealth still visible in splendid palaces, gorgeous cathedrals and magnificent castles. But none of these can compete with the splendor of nature - meadows of wildflowers painting pockets of vibrant color between dark green forests, splendid lakes reflecting snowy mountain peaks in the early morning sunlight, small hamlets hiding behind swells of rolling hills, villages snuggled in little coves of grey-green lakes, gigantic mountains pushing their jagged rocky peaks into the sky. This itinerary could be used as a reference for planning day trips from Salzburg. Another option would be to study this itinerary, choose one of the towns which sounds most intriguing and use it as a base. However, each destination suggested has its own special personality, so try to budget the time to linger in each area. Explore the ice caves. Journey down into the salt mines. Discover your own little lake. Hike up into the mountains. Circle the lakes by ferry. Relax and soak in the spellbinding beauty of Austria.

ORIGINATING CITY   SALZBURG

This itinerary begins in Salzburg, a small city which is almost too perfect. It is like a stage setting with its maze of narrow streets, colorful medieval buildings, small squares, large plazas and dramatic churches. The Old Town is squeezed in between the Salzach River and a rocky mountain where there is an enormous castle, once the residence of the powerful prince-archbishops of Salzburg. For sightseeing suggestions refer to the itinerary "Highlights of Austria by Train and Boat", page 32.

DESTINATION I   MONDSEE-PLOMBERG   Hotel Plomberg-Eschlbock

Leaving Salzburg, drive east for about 10 miles on the Al-E14 and watch for signs for the MONDSEE exit. Just a few minutes south of the expressway, the Mondsee is the first of the lakes you explore on this itinerary. At the north tip of the lake is the town of Mondsee with its 17th-century church facing the village square. The beautiful baroque church with its twin steeples, each decorated with a matching clock, was used for the wedding scene in the "The Sound of Music". Drive up the road just behind the church and in a few minutes you will see signs for the outdoor museum MONDSEER RAUCHHAUS (Smoking House) located on a small hill behind the church. Here you will find several old, very simple farmhouses which show the early Austrian way of life. The main building is reminiscent of early American frontier log cabins. The rooms are furnished with country antiques including a lovely cradle, interesting wooden handcarved chairs, wonderful old beds and wooden tables. The smoke which rose from the open fireplace into the attic loft was used for smoking meats. While in Mondsee sample their delicious Mondsee cheese, named for the lake and the town.

After brief sightseeing in the town of Mondsee, follow the road which hugs the west shore of the lake along Highway #154 (the signs will read "St. Gilgen" and "Bad Ischl"). In about five minutes you come to the small town of PLOMBERG. This tiny community holds this evening's destination, the HOTEL PLOMBERG-ESCHLBOCK, located across the street from the lake. What a treat. Who would expect to find one of the finest chefs in Austria in a tiny hotel in a small village? The food is so fabulous that you might well decide to make Plomberg your touring base and time your daily excursions carefully so as to be "home" in time for supper. Food is definitely the emphasis here and the dining rooms are all exquisite. The bedrooms are basic but those in front have beautiful views of the lake although they can be noisy due to traffic on the road and the gaiety of departing dinner guests.

Hotel Plomberg-Eschlbock
Mondsee-Plomberg

When you decide that your waistline cannot afford another day at the Hotel Plomberg-Eschlbock, continue south along the lake and in a few minutes the road splits.   Follow the signs heading east to the ATTERSEE, a few minutes' drive away.   Upon reaching the lake follow the south shoreline for about 4 miles to WEISSENBACH and then continue north along the east rim of the lake toward STEINBACH where a small sign directs you east to ALTMUNSTER.   As the road climbs the hill, look back to see a gem of a small, onion-domed chapel which completes a "postcard pretty" picture with the lake as a background.   A twenty-minute drive first climbs up through lush forest and then drops down the other side of the pass through small farms and meadows to the TRAUNSEE.   When you reach the Traunsee turn north, tracing the lake.   In a few minutes you arrive at the old town of GMUNDEN.   Visit the SCHLOSS ORT, a tiny castle on a miniature island in the lake.   Cross the bridge on to the island and wander around the picturesque castle whose courtyard is surrounded by arcaded balconies.   One side of the courtyard leads to a pretty little chapel.

Gmunden makes a nice luncheon stop since there are many restaurants in the town. Before dining, check the ferry schedule at the pier so that you can linger over your lunch, leaving just enough time to board the wonderful old-fashioned ferry which circles the lake.   (Usually there is a boat leaving about 1:00 PM for a three-hour ride around the lake.)   If the day is nice, the boat ride is highly recommended since the Traunsee is an especially lovely lake - particularly the southern section where the heavily forested hills rise like walls of green from the water's edge.

After lunch and your "cruise", leave Gmunden following the small Highway #120 west for about 10 miles to SCHARNSTEIN where you turn south for about 4 miles to GRUNAU.   Drive through town and just after crossing the bridge look to your right and you will see the ROMANTIK HOTEL ALMTALHOF.   This is another exceptionally delightful small hotel. Not only is the chalet-style hotel filled with rustic antiques, it is also filled with the warmth and caring of the Leithner family who own and manage this small inn. Their personal touch is everywhere. Mrs Leithner is a cross-stitch artist and her handiwork is on pillows, door plaques, wall hangings, napkins, tablecloths, and little rugs. Mr Leithner is also an artist. He designed and built most of the wonderful rustic pine furniture in the bedrooms. The food, too, is very special, with most of the ingredients fresh from the garden or orchard.

Romantik Hotel Almtalhof
Grunau

The Romantik Hotel Almtalhof makes a perfect base for exploring the beautiful ALMTAL VALLEY and the CUMBERLAND WILDLIFE PARK. To begin your adventures, you do not have to go far. There is a delightful walk leading from the garden of the hotel along the banks of the Alm River. Another day, take the road south from Grunau leading through a splendid forest: the prize at the end of the road is a small jewel of a lake, the ALMSEE. There is a small inn, the GASTHOF DEUTSCHES, located beside the lake with a cheerful terrace restaurant where you might enjoy a snack. Afterwards, follow some tempting paths through the meadows that circle the lake.

When it is time to leave Grunau, retrace your steps to Gmunden, and from there follow the road along the west bank of the Traunsee for the short drive to TRAUNKIRCHEN, situated on a small peninsula that gracefully extends into the lake.   Then drive on to the south tip of the Traunsee where you leave the lake and continue south following the signs for BAD ISCHL, a spa town made famous by Franz-Josef who spent holidays here with his family.   The setting of the town is splendid.   The Ischl and Traun Rivers join in Bad Ischl creating a loop of water around the spa which is still a popular health resort.

Stop to visit Franz-Josef's hunting lodge, KAISERVILLA, located on the north bank of the Ischl river (watch for the signs as you drive into town).   Park your car and walk across a bridge to visit the lodge which is filled with hunting trophies. The house is not elaborate in design or decor, but the gardens are splendid.

Continue south from Bad Ischl through the smaller spa town of BAD GOISERN and a few minutes farther arrive at STEEG, the first town on the north end of the HALLSTATTERSEE.   Follow the road as it winds around the west side of the lake and continue a short distance on to the town of HALLSTATT.   Of all the places in Austria, none can really outshine this picturesque little village whose quaint houses cling to the hillside as it rises steeply from the blue lake.   Narrow alley-width streets twist their way up the hillside.   A small church is strategically built near the edge of the lake making a gorgeous picture as its pointed steeple reflects in the deep blue lake.   When the weather is calm, the moutains encircling the dark, still waters give a fjord-like beauty to this idyllic scene.

As you stand in the main square of Hallstatt, with your back to the lake, you will see peeking out from the left corner of the plaza the GASTHOF ZAUNER.   In summertime the hotel balconies overflow with geraniums, making the hotel even easier to spot. The Gasthof Zauner is not in any way a deluxe hotel, but it is the most attractive in Hallstatt. The entrance is through a small first floor hallway where stairs lead to the reception desk, bar and dining rooms. Your gracious host, Mr Zauner, will probably be present to greet you. The dining rooms are pleasantly decorated in a hunting motif and the food is excellent with grilled dishes the specialty of the house. Upstairs are the bedrooms; a few have some antiques, but most are extremely simple with not much style. However, they are clean and pleasant and very inexpensive. (For those who prefer all of your hotels to be in the superior to deluxe category, you could bypass Hallstatt and go directly to the Schloss Pichlarn, this itinerary's fourth destination.)

Gasthof Zauner
Hallstatt

The town of Hallstatt is small with a population of approximately 1,500, but, in spite of its size, there are many places of interest. The attraction is the setting itself - the town is built upon a shelf of land which drops down to the lake. The main square is at lake level, but the rest of the town climbs the hill with the houses built along streets that are staircases. Hallstatt is Austria's oldest town: excavations show settlement here as far back as 400 BC. There are two museums in town, and one entry ticket is valid for both. The museums contain artifacts from the early salt mining days and natural history exhibits. In addition to the museums there are two churches. A lovely one is on the main square, but the more dramatic is the Parish Church, reached by a winding staircase from the center of town. Be sure to go inside to see the beautiful altarpiece painted in the l6th century and given to the church by a wealthy wine merchant.

Hallstatt is not only a very picturesque small lakeside town, it is also a wonderful base for interesting side trips. The obvious one is the ferry that departs from the pier to some of the other towns on the lake. This is fun to do, although the lake trips are short. Another trip, just a few miles from Hallstatt, is a must - the SALT MINES. For this excursion drive to the nearby town of LAHN where you will see signs to the funicular. Park your car and take the cable car up the steep incline, where you will find at the top a restaurant on the edge of the mountain with a spectacular panorama of the lake and mountains. After a cup of coffee or some lunch, follow the signs to the salt mines. The path leads across a meadow and up a hill - about a ten-minute walk - to the main lounge where you buy a ticket and wait until your tour number is called. Then, follow the guide into what looks like a locker room where pajama-like outfits are hanging according to sizes - small, medium, large. Here you put loose scrub-suit-looking pants and tops on over your clothing. After a few laughs you continue with your guide into the tunnel. The guide will probably not speak English, but if you have visited the mining museum in Hallstatt you will certainly get the general idea of what is being said as you tag along with the group along a route which descends deeper and deeper into the earth. You will not need an interpreter when you arrive at the gigantic wooden slide worn smooth as velvet over the years, one of those placed at strategic points to speed the miners' journey underground. Those still young at heart will love the ride, but for the less adventurous, a staircase parallels the slide to the bottom where you again follow the leader as you weave through a labyrinth of tunnels. (You will quickly see why you need your guide.) Before your adventure is over, you will have conquered another slide, seen an underground lake, had an audio visual lecture on the caves (you probably won't understand a word), and walked for an hour. The tour ends dramatically. The group climbs upon a small train which consists of benchlike cars, then once all are aboard, the brake is released and the train zips down the incline for about a mile and out again into the open air. A true adventure.

Another "must" from Hallstatt is a visit to the "DACHSTEINEISHOHLE" or ICE CAVES. To reach the caves follow the road to the south end of the lake toward the town of OBERTRAUN. As you near the town, watch for the sign for the road which branches to the right to the Dachsteineishohle. The name says it all - a hole with ice in the Dachstein mountains. But it is much more. Even if caverns are not "your thing", give these a try. It is a real adventure. Park in the designated car park by the gondola building, then buy a ticket and wait your turn. There are several possibilities for ticket purchase since the gondola climbs to various stages of the mountains for the convenience of skiers and hikers. You want the Eishohle which will be well marked. When you reach the top, there is about a twenty-minute hike up a trail to the ice caves. The walk is a bit strenuous but the path is well maintained and the views as you stop to catch your breath are glorious - you have a bird's eye view of the Hallstattersee. When you reach the entrance to the caves you must wait until the guide arrives; usually a handsome, athletic "outdoorsy" type. When the group is ready you follow the leader into the cavern. At first it doesn't seem anything special. Just another enormous cave. Be patient though, because as the trail winds deeper into the earth, the walls of rock gradually become walls of ice. You enter a magic kingdom where you are surrounded by translucent, everchanging mysterious forms of ice. To enhance the scene, at the most spectacular displays the guide turns on colored lights which fade, then brighten, then shade into rainbow colors.

When it is time to leave Hallstatt drive north for a few minutes, and then west for about 6 miles to the town of GOSAU.   Here a road branches to the south to the spectacularly lovely little lake, GOSAUSEE.   Although tiny, this lake is definitely worth a side trip.   Rock walls rise straight up from the depths of the lake enclosing the dark blue waters in a majestic embrace.   The mighty peaks of the Dachstein mountains form a backdrop for this beautiful stage setting.   Try to arrive at the lake before 9:00 AM for two reasons - in early morning on a clear day the surface of the lake is like a mirror reflecting the mountains in all their glory, and in early morning the busloads of tourists have not yet arrived.   Take a walk around the lake: there is a magnificent trail which takes about an hour to complete.

After visiting the lake, return to Gosau and follow the main road west for about 9 miles watching for a road that heads south, marked #166.   The road is narrow but the views are splendid as it follows a beautiful gorge then travels over a low pass for about 15 miles to NIEDERNFRITZ and then east to RADSTADT.   Radstadt, built in the 13th century by the archbishops of Radstadt, still maintains its ancient town walls and moats.   From Radstadt continue east for about 12 miles to another medieval village, SCHLADMING.   During the Middle Ages silver and copper were both mined here, but now the town is an excellent ski resort.

Continue east from Schladming on Highway #146 to IRDNING.   Near the town's main square are signs for the SCHLOSS PICHLARN.   Located in the low hills a short drive from the village, the Schloss Pichlarn is a superb hotel - elegant and sophisticated, with a history that dates back 800 years.   This is a beautiful estate offering not only an antique filled interior but also horseback riding, swimming, hiking, fishing - almost anything your heart might desire.   The ambiance is that of a country club. The decor is formal with fancy antiques, but the staff has a country charm. The dining room is attractive and has a well trained staff who artfully serve delicious cuisine.

Schloss Pichlarn
Irdning

The Schloss Pichlarn is a resort where you can easily settle for a few days. Forget the sightseeing excursions and just relax and enjoy the many amenities of the hotel.

DESTINATION V   FUSCHLSEE - HOF   Schloss Fuschl

If you enjoy luxury, it will be difficult to climb back into your car and leave "your" estate, but another beautiful hotel is at the end of today's journey.

Leaving Irdning, follow Highway #145 northwest toward BAD AUSSEE. If you enjoy hiking and the weather is kind, there is a beautiful excursion from Bad

Aussee. About 3 miles east there is a string of lakes: a large lake- the GRUNDLSEE, a medium sized lake - the TOPLITZSEE, and a tiny lake - the KAMMERSEE.

Return to Bad Aussee and continue north on Highway #145 to Bad Ischl, then turn west to STROBL. From Strobl it is only a few miles farther to the ST. WOLFGANGSEE and a few miles more to the town of ST. WOLFGANG, deserving of a visit although in season it is jammed with tourists. The Parish Church, though small, is splendidly embellished with beautiful works of art and deserves first notice. Next, you might want to have a snack on the lakefront deck of the White Horse Inn (of operatic fame). The ferryboat docks next to the hotel. Before leaving St. Wolfgang, walk to the pier and board one of the boats which afford a circle trip of the romantic lake.

The hills rise so steeply beyond St. Wolfgang that the road ends a short distance west of the village, so you must backtrack to the main highway and then continue along the south shore of the lake to the resort town of ST. GILGEN, a beautiful little village on the west shore of the St. Wolfgangsee. The town has a delightful lakefront garden and also a picturesque medieval section encircling the main square dominated by a wonderful onion-domed church. Not only was Mozart's mother born in St. Gilgen, his sister Nannerl lived here after she was married, so mementos of the Mozart family are everywhere.

It is only a short drive into Salzburg, but if you can stretch out your holiday to include one more lake, just west of the St. Wolfgangsee is the much smaller, yet also beautiful FUSCHLSEE. On a crest of a peninsula which pokes into the lake is a delightful hunting lodge, the SCHLOSS FUSCHL. The hotel has expanded so that now in addition to the original hunting lodge there are several auxiliary buildings which contain additional guestrooms and conference rooms. The main building still has the most charm and although the bedrooms are not as elaborate as the price of the hotel might indicate, they do have beautiful lake views. There are several suites which are particularly lovely should you want to splurge. The dining room is beautiful with large windows to capture the panorama of the lake. When the weather is warm, there is also a fabulous terrace where you can soak in the sun while enjoying a view of the lake. A nature preserve surrounds the hotel, giving the option of marvelous walks in the splendid countryside.

Schloss Fuschl
Fuschlsee-Hof

Marvelous Mountains
of Tyrol & Vorarlberg

◉ Overnight Stops

★ Alternate Hotel Choices
See Hotel Section of Guide

Marvelous Mountains of Tyrol and Vorarlberg

When one hears the word "Tyrol" wonderful visions dance in the mind - lush green fields with lazy cows munching grass - their huge bells ringing with the rhythm of each step, little boys with apple cheeks wearing leather shorts held up with jaunty suspenders, little girls with blond braids dressed in gay dirndls, picture perfect villages with every small chalet decorated in geraniums, simple little churches standing on mountain ledges in isolated splendor, enormous farmhouse-barn combinations with plump down pillows dangling and airing from the windows, meadows of wildflowers stretching as far as the eye can see, powerful mountains rising like walls of granite into the sky. All this is true. And more.

Lofer

The province of Tyrol fills most of the narrow long western finger of Austria - a strip intersected by the Inn Valley and enclosed both to the north and the south by spectacular mountains. The tip of the finger of western Austria is her smallest province, Vorarlberg. Combining the two provinces for an itinerary is logical, for together they complete the entire western section of the country, and although both are similar in their Alpine beauty, each has unique attributes to offer. This itinerary weaves across western Austria following one of the most scenic routes, suggesting sightseeing along the way, and staying in inns which capture the mood and beauty of the countryside.

ORIGINATING CITY   SALZBURG

After absorbing the splendors of Salzburg, a trip to the mountains of western Austria is like the icing on the cake. Salzburg is a beautiful little city, but always filled with people. The contrast of the countryside, where most of the sightseeing is of the grandeur of nature and where you will see many fewer fellow tourists, will make this itinerary all the more delightful. For sightseeing suggestions in Salzburg refer to the itinerary "Highlights of Austria by Train and Boat", page 32.

DESTINATION I   WALD IM OBERPINZGAU   Jagdschloss Graf Recke

Leave Salzburg via Highway #E17, heading southwest, following the Saalach River. You will traverse a short segment of Germany, but you will enter Austria again almost before you have time to put your passport away. As you reenter Austria, the road winds along the river following a narrow canyon.   Suddenly giant granite peaks soar behind conical shaped hills - it is an incredibly beautiful scene.

Just before the town of LOFER (about an 8-mile drive from the border) watch for a small road leading off to the left to AU.   Follow this road which circles to the left and in a couple of minutes you come to an elegant, small, pink chapel with a shingled roof and an onion dome and with mountains rising in the background. This scene is captured on many Austrian postcards.   Peek inside to see the pristine white walls accented by a lovely altar and lots of gold trim.   Return to the main road and contine on to Lofer, an extremely picturesque old market town, with another stately onion-domed church on the main square.   Stroll through the village noting the many oriel windows and painted facades of some of the buildings.   Be tempted by a cup of coffee and a pastry at one of the inns along the river which rushes through the town.   Shopping is also an option as there are some excellent stores.   This is a favorite town for American military wives who drive over from Germany for shopping sprees.   You will find lovely sweaters (both for men and women) and an excellent selection of blouses and dirndls.   Should you do some shopping and your purchases in one store are over 1,000 shillings, you can ask for a tax refund form, retrace your drive to the border (about 15 minutes), have your form validated by the Austrian customs inspector and return to the shop for an immediate refund of the 20% tax.

From Lofer continue west to WAIDRING, a small town abounding with flowers, whose tiny square hosts a delightful fountain, and many chalet style houses - some with roofs that are weighted down by stones.

A few miles beyond Waidring is another picturesque village, ST. JOHANN, surrounded by new condominiums announcing its popularity as both a summer and winter resort.   Once through the maze of new construction, you will still find the heart of the old town with many of the houses covered in intricate, colorful paintings.   Do not spend too much time, however, because the town is not nearly as charming as the next town on the itinerary.

From St. Johann follow Highway #161 south watching for the signs to KITZBUHEL. Stop in Kitzbuhel to see this town whose beauty has made it a popular year- round destination for tourists from all over the world. Although no longer a tiny village, Kitzbuhel still maintains the aura of a picture-perfect Austrian mountain hamlet. Drive through the gates of the medieval walls which still encircle the town, then park your car and explore the town on foot. A rigid building code has worked: the buildings all still reflect the glory of their past. Except for the many tourists, you will feel you have dropped into another era - a storybook setting of gaily painted old gabled houses whose windowboxes overflow in colorful flowers.

South from Kitzbuhel along Highway #161 you pass through a wide valley of farmland and then head upward over a pass. After the summit, the road weaves downwards hugging a mountainside which drops off sharply to the right and treats you to a magnificent bird's eye view of the delightful valley below. The first town you see as you enter the valley is MITTERSILL. If you like churches you will find here not one, but *TWO* baroque churches to explore.

From Mittersill it is only about 20 miles west to WALD im OBERPINZGAU. Here at the foot of the HOHE TAUERN NATIONAL PARK is the hunting lodge of the Recke Family. On the approach to town watch carefully for a small sign on the right side of the road pointing to a lane leading up the hill to the JAGDSCHLOSS GRAF RECKE. Follow this road which climbs a small hill and weaves to the right to Count Recke's hunting lodge, beautifully positioned in a meadow. The Recke family are still very personally involved with the management of this small hotel. Do not expect a slick, sophisticated hotel with all the "cutesy" decorator touches. This hotel is exactly what it has always been - a comfortable, homey, authentic hunting lodge. Of course there were not always paying guests, this has been a more recent development, but guests have always been a big part of the home. Count Recke's grandfather used to bring his friends from Poland by train to his "little lodge" and they would hunt in their personal hunting grounds - what is now the giant Hohe Tauern National Park.   Of course, after hunting everyone was hungry and so food was important, as it is now.   The meals are plentiful and delicious, with fresh vegetables and fruits.   The bedrooms are nice, but not fancy - more like one would expect in a hunting lodge.   One of the lounges is filled with hunting trophies and intriguing photographs of the Recke family and friends.   Another small lounge is more feminine - for the women after dinner who probably gossiped while the men spoke of the day's hunt.   So relax, enjoy the marvelous meals, take hikes into the beautiful countryside, swim in the small pool, and, best of all, converse with Count Recke who is charming and can fill your evenings with fascinating stories of yesteryear.

Jagdschloss Graf Recke
Wald im Oberpinzgau

Just a few miles from the hotel, a small museum is housed in a wonderful old peasant's cottage.   The museum has an excellent collection of gems which are mined in the mountains overlooking Wald.   It is very interesting that only in this one small section of Austria have emeralds been discovered.   The fame of these beautiful stones was such that it attracted buyers from as far away as Venice to trade.   (In fact, the highest peaks are called "Gross Venediger" and "Klein Venediger" in respect of these early Venetian tourists).   In addition to the rock collection, the museum also has many other exhibits including one on how honey was produced within very old beehives (of particular interest are two beehives whose doors open showing the bees very busy with their "honeywork").

DESTINATION II **PATSCH** Hotel Grunwalderhof

As you leave Wald (or on one of your daily expeditions) visit one of the most famous sightseeing destinations in Austria, the KRIMML FALLS (Krimmler Wasserfalle), the largest in Europe. As you leave the town of Wald, the road splits. The road to the right is the old mountain pass and the road to the left is a toll road. Take the road to the left marked to GERLOS and 4 miles outside Wald the falls are visible in the distance gushing from the mountains. A few minutes after spotting the Krimml Falls, there is a parking lot on the right side of the road. From there it is about 20 minutes along a well marked path to the bottom of the waterfalls. There are lovely views along the way plus a couple of cafes should you need a little refreshment en route. There is a splendid view of the falls from below where they crash to the floor of the valley and join a river which flows on through the forest. If it is a lovely day, you might want to allocate three hours and climb the path which weaves up the mountain to higher vista points.

After seeing Krimml Falls, continue west on the highway toward Gerlos. In a few minutes you come to the toll station. Keep your stub because you will need it when you pass through the station at the other end. The road over the pass is beautiful. As you climb the mountain, the road makes a series of hairpin turns en route to the summit, then curves down the other side. As the road nears the next valley, you pass a small artificial lake on your left and then arrive at the famous high mountain ski resort of Gerlos.

From Gerlos the road crosses an open valley and then twists down through the trees to an even lower valley and the town of ZELL AM ZILLER.   Once a gold-mining center, the town still retains remnants of its past glory with a lovely parish church and its most impressive dome painted by Franz-Anton Zeiller.   Visit the church and then head north on Highway #169 for about 20 miles to the main Expressway #A12.

Travel this expressway east for about five minutes to the joint exit for KRAMSACH and RATTENBERG.   When you leave the freeway follow the signs to Rattenberg. This is a medieval walled town that rose to prominence because of its valuable salt mines.   These were exhausted in the early part of the 18th century, but now the town is famous for the production of fine glassware - a craft brought to Rattenberg by refugees from Czechoslovakia.   Rattenberg is a picturesque village.   The streets are lined with many shops selling all kinds of glass, most of which are finely engraved or etched.   You can watch the craftsmen at work and have your name or initials carved while you wait.   The prices are low and the shops will mail packages home tax free - a savings which more or less pays for the postage.

After your shopping expedition, return to the main Expressway #A12 and head west following the signs to INNSBRUCK.   Before reaching Innsbruck, make a stop in HALL, which in medieval times was one of the most important towns in the Tyrol due to the mining of that most precious commodity - salt.

Leaving Hall, it is a few minutes more to Innsbruck.   Just before entering the town of Innsbruck, watch for the branch of the freeway which heads south to the BRENNER PASS.   Take this road south and watch very carefully for your exit, PATSCH. Follow the road to Patsch and on your left will be the HOTEL GRUNWALDERHOF.   This ties in nicely with your last destination, because like the Romantikhotel Jagdschloss Graf Recke, the Hotel Grunwalderhof was also a private hunting lodge, and also owned by nobility, the Counts of Thurn.   The reception areas and lounges are filled with hunting trophies and the total ambiance is that of a mountain lodge. Some of the bedrooms have antiques, although the decor is not outstanding. What is outstanding though is the view, one of the finest in Austria. The hotel is cleverly positioned on a shelf of lovely meadow which then drops down to a valley below that is walled with enormous mountains. A delightful terrace behind the hotel is a perfect spot for soaking in the sun and the stunning view. A short walk from the terrace is the swimming pool. (Note: The Hotel Grunwalderhof has a simple rustic mood. For those who prefer luxury, only a few miles farther is the elegant, deluxe SCHLOSS HOTEL IGLS in the town of Igls - see the hotel section in the back of the guide for details.)

Hotel Grunwalderhof
Patsch

Patsch is a suburb of Innsbruck, conveniently located for sightseeing. It is just a short drive into town, but the more colorful approach is to use the funicular which descends from Igls down into the town. Innsbruck is large, but at its heart is a jewel of a city whose "olde worlde" ambiance is beautifully preserved. Park your car and stroll the main street, MARIA-THERESIEN-STRASSE, lined with mouth-watering cafes and colorful shops (unfortunately most of the shops are filled with rather tacky touristy items, but it is always fun to look). Your explorations will perhaps be hampered by the constant urge to raise your eyes upward to admire the mountain peaks which form a glorious natural backdrop.

While meandering through the Old Town in Innsbruck, be sure to stop and admire the GOLDENES DACHL (Little Golden Roof) which is an intricate balcony added to the Ducal Palace to commemorate the marriage of Maximilian I to Bianca Maria Sforza. Legend says that the gold roof of the balcony was commissioned by Duke "Friedrich the Penniless" to disprove the rumors - of his poverty. This little balcony, so colorfully painted and so intricately carved, was used as a box by privileged royal guests to view in regal grandeur festivities taking place in the square below.

Another target should be the HOFBURG PALACE, built by Maria Theresa, where you can soak up the wealth and grandeur of the Hapsburg dynasty. Pause to admire the family portraits of Maria Theresa and her children.

After your day of sightseeing in the bustling, crowded tourist center of Innsbruck, it will be blissful to return to your tranquil mountain retreat.

DESTINATION III   LECH   Hotel Arlberg

When it is time to continue your journey, take the expressway toward Innsbruck but do not enter the city. Instead, as you near the outskirts of Innsbruck, take the bypass south of the city to join up with the main Expressway #A12. At this point, continue west following the INN RIVER.

If you are a sports enthusiast, watch for a road and signs leading north a few miles beyond Innsbruck for SEEFELD, a town familiar to all as the setting for the excitement generated by two Olympic games.

After visiting Seefeld, return to the main Expressway #A12 and continue west.   In a few miles the expressway ends (hopefully it will be completed by the time you arrive).   A few miles farther you come to the town of STAMS.   A stop in Stams is certainly worthwhile to visit the splendid Cistercian Abbey that dates from the 13th century.   This abbey is most impressive (180 rooms) and has two marvelous towers crowned by onion domes.

Return to the highway and continue west for about 35 miles following signs to ST. ANTON and the ARLBERG PASS.   Park your car in St. Anton and stroll the main street which has been converted to a pedestrian mall with many fancy shops - clues to the international fame of St. Anton as a jet set ski resort.   When you leave St. Anton, do not return to the main highway, but instead follow the small road which winds along the mountain, first to the small town of ST. CHRISTOPEN, and then twists its way north over the FLEXENPASS.   Crossing the pass the first town you come to is the ski resort of ZURS.   In winter this is a bustling ski resort, but in summer it is a barren little town standing almost deserted in a treeless high mountain valley.   From Zurs the road drops farther into the valley and in a few minutes you arrive in LECH - a much more attractive village with lovely chalet style hotels and shops lining both sides of a clear stream which rushes through the town. Because of its slightly lower elevation, Lech has many more trees and warmer weather than its sister ski resort of Zurs and therefore it is both a summer and a winter resort.   Hiking is the sport in summer while in winter it is skiing.   Hotel rates are lower in summer, but winter is a paradise too.   Should you be a skier, just consider the fun of staying in Lech taking the funicular to the top of the mountain and skiing down to lunch at Zurs - the mountain lift systems all interconnect, making a giant spiderweb of skiing adventures and trails.

There are only a few very old buildings in the village - the most famous being a lovely small church dating from the 14th century.   However, most of the new construction is consistent with the Alpine motif and blends beautifully into the little valley. One of these newer, but very traditional, hotels is the HOTEL ARLBERG, splendidly positioned in a grassy meadow on a bend of the Lech River. Although not an ancient structure, the inn is oozing with elegant "olde worlde" charm. The Hotel Arlberg has been in the Schneider family for many years and they have constantly made improvements and enlargements - all done in excellent taste and with loving attention to detail. The decor exudes a sophisticated charm with all the amenities one could hope for in a deluxe resort hotel.

Hotel Arlberg
Lech

DESTINATION IV SCHWARZENBERG Hotel Hirschen

This itinerary could easily end in Lech. It is only a short drive to return again over the Flexenpass to St. Christophen and only about 20 miles farther west to BLUDENZ. Here the expressway begins and whisks you quickly into Switzerland, Germany or Liechtenstein.

However, if you are afforded time and the luxury to tarry longer, there is a section of the Vorarlberg which is extremely lovely called BREGENZERWALD. The name means "the forest near Bregenz", but it is much more. Bregenzerwald is an area of soft rolling hills, impressive walls of rocky cliffs, gentle pasturelands, the winding Bregenzer Ache River, lush forests and, best of all, picturesque villages different from anything else found in Austria.

To reach the Bregenzerwald, contine north from Lech following the Lech River as it cuts a deep gorge far below the road. In spring, waterfalls leap from many of the cliffs and make inlets into the rushing river. As you near the town of WARTH the canyon opens into a high mountain valley with meadows and farms. At Warth take the road heading west to BEZAU. The road zigzags up and over the HOCH-TANNBERG PASS, where the landscape becomes wild and barren. There are some spectacular vistas, especially near the town of NESSLEGG where lunch and views from the terrace of the GASTHOF WIDDERSTEIN are gorgeous.

From Nesslegg the road drops quickly downward to the village of SCHROCKEN, and from there you follow the valley floor, walled on both sides by lush green hills. Suddenly at SCHOPPERNAU the narrow valley spreads into an open meadow and you begin to see the colorful Bregenzerwald villages. Stop in the town of Bezau, one of the most typical of the small hamlets which dot the velvety meadows. (Even if you have previously eaten, you might enjoy a delightful meal at the GASTHOF GAMS in one of several atmospheric, antique dining rooms.) Walk around the village: there are a few cute shops, but the main attraction is the architecture and decor. Most of the buildings are shingled, most of a natural wood, but sometimes painted. Shutters, usually green, enclose the small paned windows. Look carefully at the windows - they make a beautiful picture. Peeking behind the windows are filmy white cotton curtains trimmed by an exquisite handmade border of lace. Accenting the white curtains are tied-back drapes, often in a country-French blue. Below the windows are flowerboxes of geraniums - the final perfect touch.

It is only about a five-minute drive from Bezau to SCHWARZENBERG, an even smaller hamlet - well known for dairy products. As you stroll around the village you will see a large cheese factory and in the early morning and evening the sound of cow bells ushers in the parade of cows which linger for a sip of cool water at the ancient fountain in the town square. The town is not only host to cows, but a great attraction to tourists because of the wonderful assortment of typical Bregenzerwald houses.

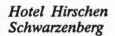

Hotel Hirschen Schwarzenberg

Your hotel, the HOTEL HIRSCHEN, is one of the finest architectural examples in town. You cannot miss the hotel - a three storied, shingled building facing the main square. When you enter the inn, immediately to the right of the hallway is found one of the most charming restaurants in Austria: beautiful mellow wooden paneled walls, tables set with blue cloths and fresh flowers, an old tiled stove, and of course - blue drapes at the windows and the fresh white curtains with the lacy trim. A welcome will be extended by the gracious owner, Mr Franz Fetz, the perfect host. Not only will he assist you with choices from his gourmet menu, but will also suggest excursions into the countryside, whether it be hiking or sightseeing. When making your reservations, ask Mr Fetz for one of his rooms furnished in antiques (there is a new wing in the back with pleasant light pine, modern decor in the bedrooms - these are nice but do not compare with the few in the front which have an antique ambiance).

In the winter Schwarzenberg is a ski resort. However, in the summertime it is equally inviting, with lovely trails just begging to be explored.

When it is time to leave Schwarzenberg, follow the small back road through Bodele down into the town of DORNBIRN.   This is a very narrow road but the scenery is splendid. The road zigzags through the mountains and then drops down into the town of Dornbirn. As you descend into the valley, the BODENSEE (Lake Constance) appears in the distance.   From Dornbirn, it is only a short drive to the highway which will lead north through BREGENZ and on into Germany or south through FELDKIRCH and into Switzerland or Liechtenstein.   If you are heading south, be sure to allow enough time to stop for at least a few hours in Feldkirch, a jewel of an ancient walled city.

Southern Lakes &
Mountains of Carinthia

⊚ Overnight Stops
★ Alternate Hotel Choices
  See Hotel Section of Guide
- - - - Suggested Side Excursion

Southern Lakes and Mountains of Carinthia

The lakes around Salzburg are beautiful. Less well known and also gorgeous are the many lakes sprinkled among the mountains of southern Austria in the province of Carinthia. Not only are these lakes beautiful, but in summertime their waters warm to a comfortable temperature for swimming - sometimes an inviting eighty degrees fahrenheit. Another plus, this patchwork of southern lakes is surrounded by majestic mountains including the mighty Dolomites whose jagged peaks line the border between Italy and Austria. The following itinerary leads you through the lake district. Although the total area is small and it would certainly be possible to base yourself in one resort and take side trips from there, each of the lakes has a special beauty and a unique character. If time allows, linger for a few days at each destination. If your time is limited, choose the lake and inn which seem most "you" and settle there. But whatever you do, try to incorporate this lovely part of Austria into your holiday.

Weissensee

Klagenfurt is easily reached by train, car or airplane, making it a convenient starting point for a trip through the lake district of southern Austria. In addition to its geographic attributes, Klagenfurt merits admiration as an interesting medieval city. Like Vienna, the medieval walls of Klagenfurt were hauled down and where they once stood a circular "ring road" now encloses the heart of the old city. At the center of these "rings" is the Neuer Platz, in the middle of which there is a statue of a marvelous old dragon - the emblem of the city. Perhaps there is some reality behind the legend of this fiery old dragon: for in Klagenfurt area a skull of an ancient rhinoceros was found - so perhaps at one time dragon-like creatures did roam these lakes and mountains. Sharing the central square with the dragon is a statue of Empress Maria Theresa. Surrounding the Neuer Platz is the old quarter with a handsome parish church, an old town hall (Altes Rathaus), the House of the Golden Goose (Haus zur Goldenen Gans), and an onion-domed Landhaus.

If you arrive early in the day in Klagenfurt, stop briefly to see the city and continue to the first destination, Millstatt. However, if you arrive too late in the day to begin your journey, stay in the old city for the night so that you can browse through the shops and enjoy the sights of this once very important medieval town. Klagenfurt does not take long to see, and a one-night stay should be sufficient. Should you decide to overnight, a hotel suggestion is the ROMANTIK HOTEL MUSIL, which is well located, just a block from the central plaza. The decor is not outstanding, but there is an interior covered courtyard which is pleasant, and best of all - a divine pastry shop.

Leaving Klagenfurt, drive directly north on Highway #83 following the signs to the airport. Five miles further on is MARIA SAAL, one of the most holy pilgrimage sites in Austria. Here in the 8th century Bishop Modestus built a church dedicated to the Virgin Mary in which many people from the surrounding area were converted and baptized into Christianity. The original structure was rebuilt in the 15th century into a stunning twin-towered Gothic church. The town, located on a small hill just a short distance to the east of the highway, is well marked. As you drive to the town you cannot help spotting the large cathedral. The road winds up the hill and you park in a little square behind the church.

Return to the main Highway #83 and continue north for a few miles watching for the exit sign for HOCHOSTERWITZ, a wonderful old castle which looks exactly as a castle is supposed to look - majestically capping a very precipitous miniature mountain and displaying a hodgepodge of turrets, thick walls and towers. This castle would certainly do justice to a fairytale. The castle is visible long before you actually arrive, and is impossible to miss. You cannot drive up, so, park your car, put on your sturdy shoes, and start your hike. It will take you about half an hour to walk to the castle, but the walk is really the essence of the castle and a sightseeing excursion in its own right. Ascending the hill, you pass through a succession of fourteen gates. These gates were designed by the most famous "castle fortification architect" of the Middle Ages and because of his skill, the castle was never conquered. You will soon see why. Each gate had its own unique brand of protection - one has holes through which hot oil was poured upon the invader, another has a moat, another a draw-bridge, another hidden spikes, another fire torch slots, etc. etc. If the enemy was clever enough to conquer one gate, he was sure to be defeated before the final entrance. Just as you draw close to the top, a path leads off to a beautiful little

chapel on a ledge overlooking the valley far below. Take the time to walk over.
Not only is the view lovely, but the church interior is splendid in its combination
of simple white walls and ornate gold altar.   Upon reaching the summit, you
will find a small museum, a central courtyard, a nice restaurant and magnificent
views.

From Hochosterwitz Castle, return to the main highway and contine north for a
few miles following the signs to ST. VEIT, the medieval capital of Carinthia.
As you approach the town you will notice the ruins of many medieval castles
which at one time guarded this strategic route to Vienna.   Upon reaching St.
Veit, follow Highway #95 west for about 14 miles to FELDKIRCHEN, at one
time an important medieval town belonging to the bishops of Bamberg.   There
is a lovely old parish church and some picturesque houses.   Continue west on a
small road following the lovely Gurk River valley. You pass through the
charming town of GNESAU with numerous weathered wooden farmhouses,
then on toward PATERGASSEN where you leave Highway #95 and head west
toward the MILLSTATTERSEE (Millstatt Lake). You pass through the
popular, rather modern, spa town of BAD KLEINKIRCHHEIM with its many
large resort hotels and continue about 13 miles farther until you see the lake.
Follow the road along the north rim of the Millstattersee to the town of the
same name, MILLSTATT.

Your hotel is not in the lakefront town, but located in a town called
OBERMILLSTATT, meaning "Upper Millstatt", exactly what it is - in the hills
above Millstatt.   Before you reach the town, watch for a sign for a road leading
up the hill to Obermillstatt.   (If you miss this sign, continue on into the town
and go to the main square where a sign indicates another small road to
Obermillstatt.) It is a very small lane which winds through the trees, then
through the meadow to the village.   This is just a tiny hamlet so should you miss
the sign or get lost, anyone should be able to point you in the right direction.
The ALPENROSE is on a knoll above the town.   Your first impression will be
that this is a deluxe new reproduction of an old farmhouse.   This is partly true,

but when you enter the lobby you will quickly identify the ancient wooden beams, weathered paneling and wonderful ceramic stove of the original farm which has recently been tastefully expanded into a small deluxe hotel. New wings have been added to include 32 beautifully decorated bedrooms and a rustic style dining room. A large patio extends the length of the hotel and on warm days it is the heart of the inn where everyone gathers to soak in the glorious view over the meadows and down to the lake. Tables are set on the deck for dining; and speaking of dining - another treat is in store in this department. The hotel features only farm fresh vegetables (straight from the hotel's own garden), homemade jams, freshly baked breads, local cheeses, fabulous cakes, pastries warm from the oven and delicious soups. In other words, the emphasis is on the food - using only the freshest and finest and healthiest ingredients. Besides eating, you can enjoy many splendid trails leading from the hotel, some to springs where you can bathe, others through the meadows and up into the hills. A short drive will also take you back into the charming old medieval town of Millstatt where you can wander through the village and then take one of the ferries which circle the Millstattersee.

Alpenrose
Millstatt-Obermillstatt

You will not want to leave the Alpenrose, but another beautiful lake and marvelous hotel await you. When you are on your way again, follow the road west along the north shore of the Millstattersee to the town of SEEBODEN and from there join the expressway heading west. Do not get too settled because you stay on the freeway for only a few minutes before leaving it to follow Highway #100 which will be marked to LIENZ. The road follows the beautiful Drau River for about 12 miles to the town of GREIFENBURG where you leave the main highway and turn south following signs to the WEISSENSEE. This is a spectacularly beautiful drive: the road curves up through beautiful green meadows and over a small pass to a high Alpine lake, the Weissensee. The first small town you will come to on the west end of the lake is TECHENDORF. As you drive through the town watch for the branch of the road to the right which crosses the only visible bridge to the opposite side of the lake. After crossing the bridge, follow the south shore of the lake and in a few minutes the road will branch. One branch leads to the lake and the other winds up the hill to the SPORTHOTEL ALPENHOF perched in the meadows above the lake.

There are many similarities between your hotel on the Millstattersee and the Sporthotel Alpenhof on the Weissensee. Both are in the hills above a lake, both specialize in gourmet dining, both feature sports activities and both are personally managed by caring owners. But there are many differences, too, which make a holiday at both a treat. Whereas the Alpenrose has a sophisticated ambiance, the Sporthotel Alpenhof has a cozy, homespun, country look. The lakes vary too. The Millstattersee is very popular, with villages dotted in almost a continuous ring around the lake. The Weissensee is still "country" - the relatively few hotels are basically converted farmhouses nestled along the lake. Except for a small village at the end of the lake, the entire eastern half of the Weissensee is a nature preserve - off limits to any commercial development. Ferries circle the lake, but they are mostly to drop off passengers who want to hike along the beautiful path which completely encircles the pristine water. The lake is an incredible emerald green color, and in the early morning and the late evening, mirrors the steep green hills which rise precipitously along its eastern half. The western half of the lake is surrounded by more gentle hills which melt down into green lawns that extend to the shoreline. There is no beach but lounge chairs dot the grass and piers extend through the reeds into the water.

*Sporthotel Alpenhof
Weissensee*

Try to extend your stay at the Sporthotel Alpenhof. A hurried visit will not do justice to its atmosphere. (During the summer season secure reservations well in advance as this is a favorite resort for the Austrians.) Those with an empathy for the rural life will love this small hotel. It is not fancy in decor, but very pleasant. Many antiques are used throughout, not with the polish of a decorator's touch, but in a way that creates homey, unsophisticated warmth that permeates the entire hotel.

If you are traveling with children they will be enthralled. The Sporthotel Alpenhof is still a farm with fields full of animals including goats which poke their heads over the fence just waiting for attention, plus the piece de resistance - a weathered wooden building filled with little boxes, or more appropriately titled chicken coops. With each room comes one's own chicken and each morning the children (and adults) walk down the path to retrieve their fresh eggs from their own chicken - a surprise adventure for all.

The Sporthotel Alpenhof offers a number of possible activities. None are of the "city sightseeing" variety, but rather, as the name of the inn hints, along a sporting theme. There is swimming in the lake, fishing, boating, tennis, and, most popular of all, hiking.

You might never want to leave your oasis of tranquility, but if the mood for sightseeing moves you to action, you can make a circle excursion to visit the old town of LIENZ. To really enjoy this outing you should allow most of the day. First leave the Weissensee and retrace the road east down into the beautiful DRAU VALLEY. At GREIFENBURG take the main highway west to Lienz. On approach, the town looks like a modern, uninteresting city. Cross the river and park at the car park near the center of the town, then walk into the heart of Lienz and you will be well rewarded. Although war destroyed much of the periphery of the town, the core has been restored to its former picturesque self. A pedestrian mall is framed by colorful buildings. There are many cafes in the square - a great suggestion for lunch would be the outdoor restaurant of the Traube Hotel. After lunch and exploring the old town, visit BRUCK CASTLE which sits on a hill above the city. This 16th-century castle, formerly belonging to the Counts of Gorz, has a museum with artifacts discovered in nearby excavations of Roman settlements, Austrian folklore and handicraft displays, and paintings by Tyrolian artists. From the castle you can look down into the city of Lienz and appreciate its lovely setting with mountains rising almost at the edge of the town.

From Lienz, return east along Highway #100 for approximately 10 miles to OBERDRAUBURG where a small road heads south and makes a series of criss-crosses as it climbs over the mountains before dropping down the other side into the next valley to the town of KOTSCHACH. From here take the Highway #111 east following the Gail River. It is a beautiful drive made all the more rewarding by glimpses to the south of the fabulous jagged peaks of the powerful Dolomites marking the border with Italy. When you reach the town of HERMAGOR, turn north again and complete your circle back to the Weissensee.

DESTINATION III   WORTHERSEE - PORTSCHACH Schloss Seefels

When it is time for you to end your lake interlude, you have several options. You can head north and over the famous GROSSGLOCKNER PASS into SALZBURG, you can drive south and be in Italy in less than an hour or you can complete your circle by returning to KLAGENFURT. If time allows one more lake interlude, retrace the highway west along the Weissensee through the town of TECHENDORF and watch for the signs for the Highway #87 going south toward HERMAGOR. At Hermagor, follow Highway #111 east toward VILLACH. A few miles before Villach, the road becomes an expressway which bypasses Villach on its way toward VELDEN. Although it requires a slight detour from the freeway, Villach is an interesting city for a short visit. It will be easy to find the center of the Old Quarter - definitely the most interesting section. Just follow the church spire and you will come to the Drau River which makes a loop outlining the ancient part of town. In the center of town on the main square is a dramatic church whose steeple soars over 300 feet into the sky. Nearby are many picturesque old houses, little shops hiding in alley- like streets, and a 16th-century Rathaus. Just a few steps from the church is the ROMANTIK HOTEL POST, an excellent choice for a luncheon stop with its gourmet restaurant. Also of interest, in the Schiller Park is a huge relief map of Carinthia. This is an especially fascinating map because it is fun to mark the mountains and lakes you have been exploring.

Schloss Seefels
Worthersee-Portschach

Leaving Villach, return to the Expressway #A2 and continue east following the signs to Velden, the popular resort and gambling center on the Worthersee. From Velden skirt the lake along the northern shore for the short drive to PORTSCHACH. Just before entering the town, on the western fringe, you will see a road heading south across the railroad tracks and a sign pointing to the right along a small lane to the SCHLOSS SEEFELS, a fancy yet tasteful lakefront resort. A wonderful place to be coddled in a lakeside manor, the Hotel Schloss Seefels has everything one could want in a deluxe resort: a spectacular indoor-outdoor pool, beautifully maintained tennis courts, swimming from a large wooden deck that extends over the lake, sunning in comfortable lounges set under the trees on a lush lawn which extends to the waterfront, water-skiing from a line of motor boats waiting for your whim, sail-surfing with an instructor ready to assist you, fishing either from the shore or one of the hotel boats, golfing just across the lake - quickly reached by motor launch. To complete the picture of perfection - the guestrooms are tastefully decorated in color coordinated fabrics, the lounges and bars are highlighted with antiques, a health spa is waiting with a masseuse, and an elegant dining room serves excellent cuisine. Although the ambiance is of sophisticated elegance, the management is anything but stuffy. You will be treated with the warmth and graciousness you have come to expect all over Austria.

When it is time to end your holiday, it is only a few minutes to Klagenfurt. From there you can continue your journey by driving north to Salzburg or Vienna, flying to your next destination or boarding one of the many express trains departing to another chapter of exciting places.

Hochosterwitz Castle

VIENNA

Bad Deutsch-
Altenburg

Hainburg

AIRPORT

Rohrau

Petronell-Carnuntum

Czechoslovakia

Bruck

Parndorf

Purbach

Hungary

Eisenstadt

Rust

Neusiedlersee

Forchtenstein

DRASSBURG

Mörbisch

Weppersdorf

Raiding

Niktch

Castles and
Wines of
Burgenland

Kroatlisch

Lutamannburg

Lochenhaus

Hungary

BERNSTEIN

Bad Tatzmannsdorf

Oberwart

Hungary

Gussing

Heiligenkreuz

Fehring

Jennersdorf

Yugoslavia

KAPFENSTEIN

SALZBURG

VIENNA

INNSBRUCK

GRAZ

KLAGENFURT

91

Castles and Wines of Burgenland

"Burg" means castle and "Burgenland" means land of the castles. The name is appropriate - Burgenland, a strip of land bordering the eastern frontier of Austria, is indeed dotted with castles. Look closely and you will spot on almost every strategic mountaintop a castle or the ruins of a once mighty fortress. This was a land of many battles. The castles were a necessity, staged against the fierce invaders from the Ottoman Empire whose dreaded warriors constantly passed through on their way to Vienna. Many of the castles are now only haunting silhouettes against the sky. Others have been converted into hotels whose rooms still hold the ghosts of days long past. Some have been turned into fascinating museums housing fabulous medieval armor.

Castles are not all that Burgenland has to offer. Here you can sample some of Austria's finest wines: this region accounts for one-third of the country's production. You can visit the wildlife sanctuary of the mysterious Neusiedler See whose waters occasionally just disappear. You can wander through the picturesque town of Rust and watch the storks feeding their little ones who peek their heads out from enormous nests on the rooftops. You can visit the castle of the powerful Esterhazy family who were the sponsors of the great musical genius, Haydn. So, if you like castles, music, wine, and "off the tourist tract" adventures, follow this itinerary for a very special treat.

ORIGINATING CITY   VIENNA

Vienna is a logical starting point for this itinerary since the boundary of Burgenland begins only a short drive from the city limits. While in Vienna soak in as much history as you can. There are superb bookstores there with a tantalizing selection of books written in English. Browse through them and buy a few - especially those dealing with the history of Austria. It will make this itinerary "come alive" as you later wander through Roman encampments, visit castles filled with weapons used against the invading Turks, and explore palaces owned by the wealthy Esterhazy family whose power rivaled that of the Emperor. Pick up too a book on the music of Austria, an especially good one is Richard Rickett's "Music and Musicians in Vienna". As you later follow the trail of Haydn and Liszt (both sons of Burgenland) you almost hear the haunting melody of their music when you visit their homes.

Absorb as much history as you can from the tour guides who take you through Maria Theresa's palaces. Ask about how this determined "Child Queen" wrested power from the princes whose small kingdoms in Burgenland almost rivaled her own. Attend as many musical performances as you can. The lives of all of Austria's musicians mesh together and much of it originated with the genius of Haydn who attributed the originality of his music to the fact he was for so many years isolated in Burgenland where he could not copy the popular musical trends.

While in Vienna there are several excellent hotel choices. Read the hotel section in the back of this guide to see which appeals most to your style and budget. Try to plan well in advance since Vienna is a very popular tourist destination and hotel space is always at a premium.

DESTINATION I   DRASSBURG   Schloss Drassburg
===

Try to get an early start today because there are many places of interest to see en route. Leaving Vienna, take the Expressway #A4 which follows the Danube east. It is an easy route to find - just follow the Airport signs. The expressway ends but a good road continues on toward the Hungarian border. About 15 miles beyond the airport you will come to PETRONELL-CARNUNTUM where signs on both sides of the road indicate footpaths to Roman ruins. There is now only a hint at what was once a stronghold of the Roman power in Austria: only a couple of amphitheaters located in open meadows, some ruins of Roman houses, and a lonely stone gate remain. (To see what was found in the excavations, continue on a few miles farther to the town of BAD DEUTSCH-ALTENBURG where most of the artifacts are displayed.) Although the excavation site is not dramatic, the Romans played such an important role in Austria's history that it is good to soak in a bit of the mood - plus the walk through the fields to the amphitheaters is very pleasant. A few miles farther east, almost on the border of Czechoslovakia, is the medieval walled city of HAINBURG. If you are short on time, skip this stop: although it still maintains its circle of ramparts, there are more beautifully maintained medieval towns to see. Nevertheless, if time allows, do drive through because the town of Hainburg was one of the most important ancient cities of Austria and many famous battles were fought here.

Leaving Hainburg, retrace your drive and return west along the Danube for about 5 miles, returning to Bad Deutsch-Altenburg where you take the road south. In a few minutes you will arrive in ROHRAU. Just before you enter the town, watch on the left side of the road for the simple white thatched cottage where Haydn was born: his birthplace is now a small museum. It will take only a few minutes to see the few rooms. Of special interest are the many pictures of his fellow musicians. Just a few minutes beyond Haydn's birthplace, you will see on the right side of the road a large palace dramatically surrounded by superb gardens. This estate ties in with Haydn's life as his mother was a cook for the wealthy Harrach family who were, and still are, the owners of this castle. But far more than the fact that Haydn's mother worked here, the castle is worth a stop because now it also houses one of the finest private art collections in Austria, the HARRACH GALLERY. Park your car, and walk into the courtyard to buy your ticket to the museum. More than 200 paintings representing artists from all over the world are elegantly displayed in light airy rooms. Don't miss a long corridor whose walls are lined with huge murals depicting famous Austrian battles. It is fascinating to see the battle formations and the homey touches such as women cooking the meals, children frolicking just behind the field of battle, and dogs following their masters. Note especially the dress and weapons - you will be seeing the real thing a little later on in this itinerary at Forchtenstein Castle.

Continue south from Rohrau and when you reach BRUCK AN DER LEITHA, head east for about 4 miles to PARNDORF. Here take the main road south and in a few minutes you will see ahead of you the NEUSIEDLER SEE. Some of Austria's finest wines are grown in the fertile marshy lowlands stretching around the lake.

The Neusiedler See is intriguing. About once a century there is NO lake - it simply disappears. And then, for no apparent reason, it comes back again. There are almost no tributaries into the lake - the source of water seems to blossom forth from underwater springs. Another strange occurrence is that sometimes the lake shifts - rather like a tilting cup of water. When this takes place, land is quickly claimed, but before the arguments of possession are solved, the water usually shifts again and the land is recaptured by the mischievous lake. In spite of its naughty nature, the lake is fascinating: so shallow that a man can usually stand and keep his head above water, and so encumbered with reeds that long piers must extend out from the shore for access. Its very nature welcomes birds, and this is a paradise for the bird watcher - more than 250 species of birds, protected by law, make this their home.

The road splits as it approaches the lake. Keep on the main road which follows the western shore. A few miles beyond the town of PURBACH, a small road heads south to RUST, a charming village with picturesque old houses, many still with thatched roofs. Park your car in the center of the town and wander around. Look carefully and you will see storks proudly perched on their rooftop nests. If you are lucky, you might even see a baby stork noisily asking for dinner. In addition to having quaint architecture and roofs decorated with storks, Rust also produces some of Austria's loveliest wines. On little streets leading off from the central plaza, you will frequently see evergreen branches tied above arcaded doorways, indicating a simple wine tavern within, where the owner serves his own wine. Step into the inner courtyard and sit down at one of the wooden tables for a bite to eat and a sample of the famous Rust wine. See if you agree with the Hungarian prince who was so fond of Rust's vintage that he gave the town the stamp of royalty.

A few miles farther south along the lake you come to the town of MORBISCH, not quite as colorful as Rust but also picturesque with many little lanes spanned by arcades which connect gaily painted houses.

After meandering through Rust and Morbisch, take the road west to EISENSTADT. This town where Haydn lived for 30 years is full of mementos of his musical genius. The young Haydn was sponsored by the Esterhazy family. The powerful Princes of Esterhazy, who incidentally claimed descent from Attila the Hun, were an immensely wealthy, powerful family in Burgenland and Hungary, their holdings rivaling those of the Emperor, and at times their wealth surpassed his. It was a popular concept for wealthy nobles to have their own court musician, and Haydn was hired to lead the musical life at the SCHLOSS ESTERHAZY. You cannot miss the castle, a large imposing structure on one of the main streets with gardens stretching behind. Park your car and walk into the lobby to check the time of the tours (you cannot wander about on your own). Usually the tours leave about once an hour, on the hour. If you have to wait for your tour, buy your tickets and take the short walk to the simple home only about a block away where Haydn lived for 30 years. As you face the castle, the street where Haydn lived runs along the right side of the castle grounds. Follow this street and you will find his small house on the left side of the road, #21 Haydngasse, marked with a plaque. There is an appealing small courtyard but the house is not grand. Inside the rooms are simple - mostly showing some interesting photographs both of Haydn and also his musical contemporaries. Near the piano a tape plays some of Haydn's delightful compositions. It is almost like magic - you feel he has returned and is playing especially for you.

Be sure also to take the tour of Schloss Esterhazy. The castle itself has become a bit dilapidated, but painting and restoration are in progress and it might be transformed to its previous glory by the time you arrive. But even if not, by all means take the tour. The lecture will probably be in German, but if you buy a small pamphlet in English at the ticket desk, you will understand the gist of what is being said. Actually you do not need to understand much - the tour is self-explanatory. You will see several of the rooms where Haydn worked, including the highlight of the tour, the Haydn-Saal, a huge concert hall decorated with 18th-century frescoes. It was here that Haydn entertained the Esterhazy family and their friends almost every evening, usually with his own masterful compositions.

The Esterhazy family constantly desired new pieces which motivated Haydn to compose a stream of superb music. As mentioned previously, Haydn attributed his new breath of originality to his isolation in Eisenstadt where he could not copy the stilted music so popular in Vienna.

Schloss Drassburg
Drassburg

From Eisenstadt follow Highway #331 south for about 7 miles watching for a small road heading east to DRASSBURG, your destination for the night. As you drive into town, the SCHLOSS DRASSBURG is down a small lane to the left of the main road. The Schloss Drassburg is a gentle 14th-century castle - not a foreboding structure on the top of a hill, but rather a stately manor house set in vast acres of gardens. The grounds are spectacular - they were laid out by the same landscape architect who designed Versailles. Although they do not have their original grandeur (it would cost a fortune in upkeep), they are still wonderful, filled with terraces, pools, secret gardens, gazebos, hidden pathways, trellises, statues, fountains - a true fairyland to explore. The hotel is still the home of the Baroness Maria Patzenhofer, your gracious hostess. What fun it is to study the many family photographs and see the Baroness and her family as they partied in the garden and rode horseback through the forests. The rooms at the castle vary. Most of them are decorated in antiques and although the ambiance is splendid, the furnishings are quite formal and sometimes a bit worn.   However, the service is absolutely superb, the atmosphere delightful, the linens of the finest quality, and the food delicious - the Baroness has taught the talented cook to prepare family recipes. Try to spend several days in this little-known nook of Austria just on the Hungarian border.   There is plenty to keep you occupied: an indoor pool, an outdoor pool, a sauna, riding stables, tennis (the courts did not look in perfect condition), and of course walks through the lovely grounds - 25 acres of parklike beauty.

DESTINATION II   BERNSTEIN   Burg Bernstein

When it is time to leave Schloss Drassburg, retrace your steps to Highway #331 and turn south for a few miles to MATTERSBURG at which point you take another road west for a few miles to FORCHTENSTEIN CASTLE.   You should not get lost because not only is the castle well marked by signs, it also can be seen from far away dominating the top of a hill. The approach road to the castle twists up the mountain to the car park at the summit.   If you time your arrival for lunch, there is a restaurant on the cliff next to the castle with a stunning view of the valley.   By all means take the tour.   This castle, originally built by the powerful Mattersburg family and then later rebuilt by the Esterhazy family, was a key defense against the terrible Turks.   The castle is still in fabulous condition.   In the museum you see the original equipment used by the Esterhazy army.   It is a dazzling display - the largest private collection of armor in Europe.   Even the Tower of London with its enormous military museum is not much more impressive.   In fact, the museum of Forchtenstein is in some ways even more interesting because it is more personalized.   You walk through enormous rooms where the equipment was kept - one complete room of helmets, another of spears, another of saddlebags, etc. What a dramatic reminder of the power, wealth and splendor of the Austrian nobility. The armory is not all there is to see at Forchtenstein Castle.   The kitchen is also very interesting with its giant spit over an open fire - seemingly large enough to roast meat for an army, which it probably did. In the courtyard there is a well over 400 feet deep which was dug by some of the less fortunate Turks who were captured and had to work as slaves. Also on display are other mementos of the battles with the Turks: you will see many captured weapons and, most interesting of all, a wonderful Turkish tent, probably used by the commanding officer. In one of the corridors of the castle is an assortment of elaborate coaches and sleighs used by the Esterhazy family. All in all, a wonderful museum.

Leaving Forchtenstein Castle, return east to the main Highway #331 and continue south for about 10 miles to WEPPERSDORF where a small road heads east for about 3 miles. Then turn south to RAIDING, the birthplace of another musical genius, FRANZ LISZT. His home is now a museum, the walls covered with musical mementos and photographs. It is interesting to see the photographs of many of Austria's musical masters - many of whose lives were interwoven. In the lobby is a small shop where you can purchase literature and musical tapes.

After a visit to Liszt's birthplace, follow the maze of little roads heading in a southeasterly direction toward the Hungarian border; then trace the border road through the little wine hamlets of NIKTSCH-KROATLISCH-LUTAMANNSBURG and then on to LOCHENHAUS, another of Burgenland's lovely hilltop castles. The castle has a nice restaurant in the central courtyard plus an adjacent indoor tavern-like restaurant. You might want a snack or a cold drink in the courtyard before a visit to the small museum.

From Lochenhaus it is only a few minutes to the main Highway #50 where you turn south following the signs for BERNSTEIN. This is your destination for the night so as you drive through town watch for a sign on the right side of the road leading up the hill to the hotel, BURG BERNSTEIN. As you approach the dramatic fortress-like castle you park your car outside the walls and walk through the gates into the inner courtyard. The hotel is owned and managed by the Berger family, and Andree Berger will probably be there to greet you and show you to your room. And what rooms they are! Most are splendid big rooms with magnificent museum-quality antiques. When the castle was transformed into a hotel, the original furniture was retained. Because of this, the rooms vary tremendously, but all are interesting. You might find yourself in a giant room with a bathtub tucked into the corner behind elegant drapes or a formally splendid room with severe ancestors peering at you from their frames of gold. Or your bedroom might have a balcony which opens onto the ramparts of the castle. No matter which room you have, it will be fun. Do not expect spiffy decorator touches: this castle is authentic and the furniture speaks its own message of bygone days - no cute touches needed to set the mood. The dining room is outstanding - a large room with a lavishly detailed baroque ceiling and frescoes ornamenting the lovely alcoved windows.

Burg Bernstein
Bernstein

There is a wide choice of activities while staying at the Burg Bernstein: you can hike or swim in the pool or hunt in the castle's private hunting grounds. Enquire about the jade carvings and jewelry which come from Bernstein.

This itinerary stretches its boundaries a little. SCHLOSS KAPFENSTEIN is actually not in Burgenland, but about 3 miles over the border in the province of Styria (Steiermark). However, since this is one of the loveliest castle hotels in Austria (which didn't quite fit into any other itinerary), it is included.

As you leave Bernstein continue south along Highway #50. In a few miles you will come to the popular health spa of BAD TATZMANNSDORF. The town is not very interesting and quite crowded with tourists "taking the waters", but there is a splendid park in the center of the town which you might want to see.

Drive south from Bad Tatzmannsdorf on Highway #50 which becomes Highway #37 near the town of OBERWART. The scenery becomes more beautiful the closer you get to the Hungarian border. The rolling hills are covered with farmland, and peasant women work in the fields gathering the wheat, bright scarves tied around their hair. Occasionally you see a thatched-roof cottage. When you reach the town of GUSSING, a large 12th-century castle dominates the crest of a hill overlooking the village on the right side of the road. This picturesque castle is open to the public and affords splendid views of the valley and the mountains. From Gussing, it is only about 7 miles to the Hungarian border.

Beyond Gussing you come to HEILIGENKREUZ where your way becomes a little tricky. Head west along a small road toward the town of JENNERSDORF and follow the Raab River for about 6 miles to the town of FEHRING where a road goes south to KAPFENSTEIN. This area is glorious and tonight's hotel, the Schloss Kapfenstein, captures the beauty. As you wind up through fields of vineyards and past a beautiful little chapel to the 12th-century castle, you will get a hint of the views which will come into their fullest glory at the summit of the hill.

You will not be disappointed. The hotel is bounded by a romantic wide terrace and intimate little gardens with breathtaking views. Looking to the left you see Hungary, looking to the right you see Yugoslavia. Many of the well furnished bedrooms also afford beautiful vistas. Although the views are truly spectacular, the Schloss Kapfenstein offers much more - gracious owners, the Winkler family, who personally tend to the guests' every need, a fabulous restaurant serving only the finest fresh foods, a pleasant decor incorporating many antiques, and a delectable choice of wines prepared from the castle's own vineyards.

Schloss Kapfenstein
Kapfenstein

The Schloss Kapfenstein will not be everyone's cup of tea: the location is remote, the hotel has no schedule of planned activities, and there are no televisions or telephones in the rooms. But for those whose hearts pine for perfect tranquility, peaceful walks through vine-covered fields, moments of solitude in a lovely garden, the joy of reading in the sunshine on the terrace - for those of you, the Schloss Kapfenstein will be perfection.

HOTEL MAP INDEX

Austria

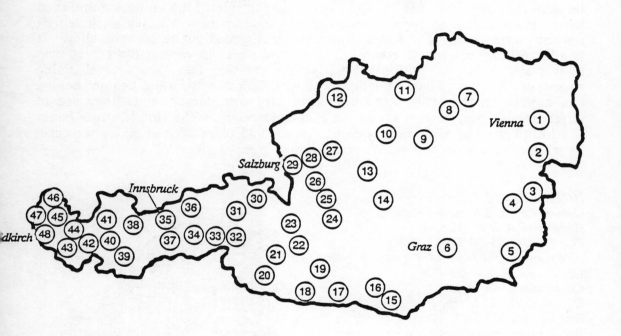

Map of Austria Showing Hotel Locations

As we approached the town of Badgastein it looked hopelessly big and commercial with factories followed by wall-to-wall huge Victorian spa hotels.   But luckily we continued on, following the signs to the Hotel Gruner Baum.   The road weaves through the town, over the roaring river, hugs the side of the mountain and then leaves Badgastein and curves down into a gorgeous narrow valley encircled by towering mountains.   The Hotel Gruner Baum is spread out across this valley.   It is a large hotel but the 95 rooms are scattered about in various old chalet-style houses and cottages.   Within the village-like complex there are several dining rooms: one has a cozy hunting lodge motif with dark paneled walls, beamed ceiling and antlers on the walls.   The bedrooms vary considerably since they are in different buildings, but they are all pleasant and modern.   The Hotel Gruner Baum is a health spa and in summer seems to cater to an older clientel taking the cure. In winter I am sure the more robust skiing group arrives.

HOTEL GRUNER BAUM
Owner: Family Linsinger-Blumsche
Badgastein A-5640, Austria
Tel: (06434) 25160 Telex: 67-516
95 Rooms - Dbl from AUS 1,040 to 2,400
Open: mid May - mid Oct
Credit cards: All major
U.S. Rep: David Mitchell
Rep tel: 800-372-1323
Beautiful mountain valley setting
Located 100 km S of Salzburg

If the thought of slipping back through the ages and living in an authentic romantic castle appeals to you, then I highly recommend the Burg Bernstein.   It has everything one dreams of in the castle department - enormous rooms, priceless antiques, a hilltop setting, towers, turrets, an old well, a prehistoric museum and even a resident ghost.   The ghost is the wandering spirit of a beautiful young woman - the wife of a medieval owner of the castle.   Her husband became grouchy when he discovered she was in love with her music teacher.   For her indiscretion he promptly walled her up in her room to die.   But she is a friendly ghost and you will never be bothered in the comfort of your bedroom - and what rooms they are.   A few are just large bedrooms, but most of the accommodations are suites.   Our suite consisted of a huge living room, a tiny sun room, an enormous bedroom PLUS a bathtub in the corner of the room artfully hidden behind a curtain hanging from an antique four-poster bed.   Meals are served in the courtyard or in a splendid dining room where frescoed walls decorate the deeply recessed windows and ornate plasterwork enhances the ceilings.   Sometimes dinner is accompanied by music - the night of our stay a talented group played chamber music.

BURG BERNSTEIN
Owner: Family Berger
Bernstein A-7434, Austria
No telephone
10 Rooms - Dbl AUS 800
Open: Easter through Sep
Credit cards: AX DC
Wonderful hilltop castle
Located 100 km S of Vienna

The history of the Gasthof Gams dates back to 1648 when it was built as a homestead for the Feuerstein family, although its age could not be determined from the rather drab exterior.   From the time of its first occupant the Gams has operated as a Gasthof and inside the atmosphere takes on the character and flavor of its past and the love its successive generations of innkeepers have lavished becomes readily apparent.   On each side of the rather plain second floor entrance hall are a series of individually styled, superbly decorated dining rooms in antique decor.   Happily, the cuisine is delicious and its excellence complements the beauty of its surroundings.   At the rear of the hotel is a glass-enclosed terrace which overlooks a garden where lounge chairs are set out near the pool, beyond which are tennis courts. The inn has 40 bedrooms, which vary from modern to the more traditionally decorated rooms found in the older section of the hotel.   The Gams is being renovated, modernized and restored on an ongoing basis.   In 1904 the great festhall with its baroque ceiling designed by local artists was added.   Although the original Feuerstein family name was lost through marriage in 1900 as there were no more heirs, the Nenning-Kaufmann family are direct descendants.   The entire family takes pride in combining the modernization with the old tradition of the hotel.

GASTHOF GAMS
Owner: Family Nenning-Kaufmann
Bregenzerwald
Bezau A-6870, Austria
Tel: (05514) 2220 Telex: 59144
40 Rooms - Dbl from AUS 680 to 1,040
Closed: Dec 1 - 15 and Apr 11 - 28
Credit cards: None accepted
Especially famous as restaurant
Located 70 km E of Feldkirch

The Alpenhotel Bodele is located on a small back road winding through the mountains from Schwarzenberg to Dornbirn. The hotel is admirably positioned above the road on a small plateau with a choice view of meadows, forests and mountains. The core is a weathered chalet, its wooden, weather-darkened balconies laden with geraniums. To either side of the original chalet, new wings have been added, and although new, the construction has been accomplished with meticulous care to detail - even the old balconies have been perfectly duplicated. A wide terrace sweeps around the side of the building. Inside, there is an airy reception lounge with an inviting fireplace - a cozy spot to gather after skiing. To the left of the lobby is a very large dining room decorated with lovely taste. Although the light pine furniture is new, it maintains the mood of the mountains with a rustic country feel. One nook of the dining room has been cleverly incorporated within a small glass-enclosed terrace - a sunny bright room just perfect for breakfast. Upstairs the bedrooms are enormous. All are actually suites, frequently with a separate sitting area with a couch that makes into an extra bed. Again, the furniture is light pine in keeping with the country look of a mountain chalet. For ski enthusiasts, the hotel offers another bonus - handsome Marc Girardelli, the owners' son, winner of both silver and bronze medals in the 1985 World Cup championships.

ALPENHOTEL BODELE
Owner: Family Girardelli
Bodele A-6850, Austria
Tel: (05572) 7250
17 Rooms - Dbl AUS 1,000
Closed: spring and autumn
Located in western Austria near Dornbirn

"I keep my house in the ancient Austrian family tradition, which preserves the good, and where the world is still in order. It is the most distinguished duty for me and my staff, to conserve this atmosphere and transmit it to my guests." Such noble ideals set forth by the owner, Baroness Maria Patzenhofer, reflect the very special quality of this castle hotel, her ancestral home, located only a few kilometers from the Hungarian border. It is a beautiful property. The grounds are perhaps the most distinctive feature of this once glorious estate, 24 acres of gardens, secret passages, statues, hidden ponds, orchards, and winding walkways. Although I saw three gardeners trimming and manicuring the grounds, it seems they only hint at their former grandeur. I think it would take at least a dozen such fellows to keep the estate in perfect condition. It is no wonder the grounds are laid out so beautifully - the plans were drawn up by the same architect who designed Louis XIV's gardens at Versailles. Inside the decor is one of a formal, somewhat faded elegance. The food is fabulous. When I complimented the Baroness on the quality of her meals, she said the chef was a young lady who had been with her for many years and whom she taught the art of preparing her family's treasured recipes.

SCHLOSS DRASSBURG
Owner: Baroness Maria Patzenhofer
Drassburg A-7021, Austria
Tel: (02686) 2220
35 Rooms - Dbl from AUS 720 to 1,120
Open: Mar - Nov
Credit cards: DC
Swimming pool, tennis, horseback riding
Located about 50 km S of Vienna

Schloss Durnstein is a magical castle in a fairytale village. This superb castle hotel, dating from 1630, is blessed with a dazzling location, high on the cliffs overlooking one of the most beautiful scenes in Austria - the Danube river weaving its way toward Vienna through some of Austria's finest vineyards. A garden is tucked into the walls of the castle. From the garden a "secret" staircase tunnels through the cliffs to the banks of the Danube - most convenient for guests taking the ferry. Also within the garden is a captivating terrace restaurant with tables set under the trees for dining: you can sit for hours happily sipping delicious local wine and watching the river traffic. But it is not just the setting or the view which makes the Hotel Schloss Durnstein so special: the management is friendly and efficient, the food is a gourmet delight, the antique decor is beautiful, the wines are delicious, and there is a lovely swimming pool attractively built into an intimate protected patio. The lounges and the guestrooms have a formal elegance, but the mood of this hotel is not stuffy: a warmth and graciousness prevail.

SCHLOSS DURNSTEIN
Owner: Johann Thiery
Durnstein A-3601, Austria
Tel: (02711) 212 Telex: 71147
37 Rooms - Dbl from AUS 1,500 to 2,200 *
  * Rate includes 2 meals
Open: Mar 25 - Nov 8
Credit cards: All major
U.S. Rep: Dial Austria
Rep tel: 800-221-4980
Swimming pool, view of Danube
Located on Danube W of Vienna

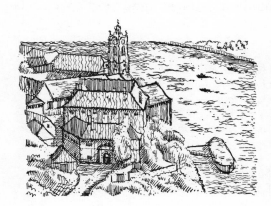

In addition to being a lovely medieval village along the Danube, Durnstein is also famous because England's King Richard the Lionheart was imprisoned in the castle on the hill above the town.   The castle is now in ruins, but the romantic story of how the King was rescued by his faithful minstrel, Blondel, still lingers on.   Named in memory of this famous king, the hotel was once a monastery and like so many old church properties it occupies the "choice" site in town.   Its ancient monastic walls are still standing and today they enclose one of the nicest features of the hotel - a lovely swimming pool and a beautiful garden.   The hotel is perched high on a cliff overlooking the Danube with a fabulous view and, to capture the beauty, there is a terrace which stretches to the side of the hotel - a favorite place for guests to sit and sip some of the local wine and watch the boat traffic on the river, far below.   In addition to the terrace dining area, there is an enclosed small adjacent restaurant, plus another large one within the main building.   There are some antique furnishings in the public rooms.   The ambiance is one of a dignified hunting lodge with heavy furniture and trophies on the walls.   The bedrooms are pleasant, but modern, with nothing very spectacular about their decor.

HOTEL RICHARD LOWENHERZ
Owner: Raimund Thiery
Durnstein A-3601, Austria
Tel: (02711) 222 Telex: 071199
36 Rooms - Dbl from AUS 990 to 1,570
Open: Mar - Oct
Swimming pool, view terrace
Monastery converted to hotel
Located on Danube W of Vienna

In every book there are a few favorites - inns that incorporate all the ingredients for a perfect little hotel. The Hotel Alpenrose is such an inn. One of the reasons this hotel is so special is the charm of the owner, Mrs Gutwinski, who orchestrates her establishment with grace and skill. She radiates charm and speaks excellent English. In addition to her friendly management, the hotel has many other attributes: it is conveniently located (on a small side street just a block from the heart of Feldkirch), it is very old (dating back to 1550), it is very small (only 16 bedrooms), and it has many antiques (most inherited from Mrs Gutwinski's grandmother who originally owned the hotel). The guestrooms are quite charming - not deluxe but furnished with loving care and with a few well chosen antiques. Each room is different, but each nice in its own way. As I walked around, it seemed as though I was visiting in a private home rather than staying in a hotel. There is a small square in front of the hotel; then as you enter, an intimate lobby with a small breakfast room to the left. Breakfast is the only meal served - and I might add it is served splendidly on fine china. Lunch and dinner are no problem since there are many excellent restaurants close by. (A very famous restaurant, the Baren, is only a few blocks away.)

HOTEL ALPENROSE
Owner: Family Hefel Gutwinski
Rosengasse 6
Feldkirch A-6800, Austria
Tel: (05522) 22175
16 Rooms - Dbl from AUS 600 to 730
Open: All year
Credit cards: MC VS
Beautiful small hotel
In the center of Feldkirch
Located near the Swiss Border

Walk back in time through the arched stone doorway leading to the interior court-yard of the Gasthof Deim zum Goldenen Hirschen.   Dating from 1442, and filled with antiques and artifacts, this is an atmospheric inn which overflows with charac-ter and history.   Wolfgang Deim is the hospitable owner who oversees all aspects of the Gasthof Deim, as his family has done for three generations.   We found him supervising the friendly, bustling restaurant where many local families were enjoy-ing a late breakfast.   Delicious meals and large steins of thirst-quenching beer are served here on wooden tables amidst stone pillars which support the low, arched and beamed ceiling.   A particularly pretty old ceramic stove warms the restaurant on cold days, and in warm weather guests are served on the lovely garden terrace. Bedrooms are reached by walking through the flower-filled interior courtyard and hallways that are decorated with antiques and old prints.   Good taste prevails in the rooms, which are furnished in a contemporary country style.   Herr Deim's artistic flair and love of history are evident throughout, from strategically placed jugs of flowers to an old apple wine press and sauerkraut cutter displayed in a stone corridor.   If you are visiting the historical walled town of Freistadt, the Gasthof Deim should not be missed.

GASTHOF DEIM ZUM GOLDENEN HIRSCHEN
Owner: Wolfgang Deim
Bohmergasse 8
Freistadt A-4240, Austria
Tel: (97942) 2258 or 2111
23 Rooms - Dbl from AUS 700 to 1000
Closed: 2 weeks end of January
Credit cards: DC
Restaurant with garden seating
Located 40 km N of Linz

Fulpmes is situated in a lovely, long and narrow Alpine valley located high above Innsbruck.   Take the Brenner road out of Innsbruck, but do not take the freeway. Instead, enjoy the beautiful winding drive up through forested hillsides, opening up onto high meadowlands.   The unfolding scenery will undoubtedly prompt many photos, for it is breathtaking and picturesque.   Continue past the first part of Fulpmes, through a covered wooden bridge to the "Ortsteil Medraz".   Signs will direct you to turn left to find the Hotel Pension Auenhof.   The Auenhof is a newer chalet, but built in the old style.   The guest sitting area contains appealing antique painted furniture, Oriental rugs, and a collection of clay pipes mounted on the wall. One can easily imagine skiers playing cards at the table in front of the fireplace after a day on the nearby slopes.   The dining room is pretty, with carved wooden chairs and benches upholstered in muted tapestry colors, fresh flowers and plants and a spectacular view through picture windows of rolling hills, pine trees and an impressive glacier.   Guests may choose from three set dinner menus, all appealing and offering regional cooking.   The 24 bedrooms can be reached by elevator or the main staircase.   These rooms all have private toilet and shower and are comfortable and functional in their furnishings.   The highlights of this inn are its antique filled public areas and the surrounding Tyrolean countryside.

HOTEL PENSION AUENHOF
Owners: Karl & Edith Volderauer
Fulpmes-Medraz A-6166
Austria
Tel: (05225) 2763
24 Rooms - Dbl AUS 640
Open: All year except Nov
Credit cards: None accepted
Located 15 km SW of Innsbruck

The location of the Schloss Fuschl is spectacular: a wooded knoll overlooking a small, beautiful lake, the Fuschlsee. There are 90 rooms - 23 in the original castle which dates back to 1540 and the others scattered about in newer additions and lakefront bungalows. Many of the bedrooms in the old section of the hotel have lovely lake views. Though not outstanding, these rooms are pleasantly decorated in muted colors with modern furniture and nice prints on the walls. The suites are very large, decorated in antique, though somewhat fussy, decor. The bathrooms are large and well equipped. The lounge has vaulted ceilings, a large fireplace, Oriental rugs, and exquisite tapestries. The dining room is especially inviting, decorated in soft pinks and tans and enclosed on three sides by picture windows that capture the magnificent lake panorama.

SCHLOSS FUSCHL
Owner: Max Grundig
Hof bei Salzburg
Fuschlsee A-5322, Austria
Tel: (06229)22530 Telex: 633454
90 Rooms - Dbl from AUS 2,000 to (Apt) 4,000
Open: end Mar - mid Nov
Credit cards: AX DC VS
U.S. Rep: David Mitchell
Rep tel: 800-372-1323
Pool, tennis, golf, lake
Overlooking small lake
Located 25 km E of Salzburg

As you drive into the small mountain village of Gerlos, you cannot miss the Hotel Gaspingerhof - it is located on the main highway next to the church.   The hotel is actually on both sides of the road with the annex connected to the main hotel by an underground tunnel.   There is a patio with tables for dining in front of the hotel. As you enter, you will find a lobby with many beautiful antiques and artful arrangements of fresh flowers.   All the Horl family is actively engaged in the management of the hotel and so if it is the dinner hour Mr Horl will probably be overseeing the kitchen, while his mother or sister will probably be there to greet you.   There are several dining rooms serving excellent food and in one there is a wonderful antique rattan sleigh filled with flowers.   The nucleus of the inn is very old, dating back to the 17th century when the inn was a postal stop.   Now only the core is old since the Horl family, who have owned the hotel for three generations, have added on extensively.   However, they have cleverly maintained an "olde worlde" ambiance with the extensive use of family heirlooms and more recent antique acquisitions.   Their old painted armoirs and wedding chests are amongst the most beautiful that I saw in Austria.   The bedrooms do not have antique furnishings but are modern and attractive.   There is also an indoor swimming pool and sauna.

HOTEL GASPINGERHOF
Owner: Family Horl
Gerlos A-6281, Austria
Tel: (05284) 5216 Telex: 54167
25 Rooms - Dbl AUS 412
Indoor pool and sauna
Town famous for skiing
Located SE of Innsbruck

Loving care shows through in every detail of the Hotel Seehof - such as family heir-looms artistically arranged in glass display cases, one with great grandmother's dirndl complete with hat and scarf, another with great grandfather's Sunday outfit complete with leather britches, fancy hat and marvelous old pipe. The oldest room in the house is a fabulous old paneled dining room, now used only for very special occasions. To the rear of the house there is a cheerful lounge, completely modern in decor, but bright and airy. The dining room is also modern. Under a large shade tree behind the hotel, tables and chairs invitingly dot the lawn which stretches down to a small lake where guests swim in summer. The bedrooms are all most attractive with stark white walls accentuated by charming watercolor prints by the Swedish artist Carl Larsson. Most of the bedrooms have modern furniture but my favorites were the few with antique handpainted chests and beds. The Schellhorn family has owned the inn for four generations. Mrs Schellhorn is the chef and a most talented one - the food is delicious. Should your holiday be in late June, you might be able to sample some tiny succulent fresh wild strawberries - freshly picked from the forest.

HOTEL SEEHOF
Owner: Family Schellhorn
Goldegg am See A-5622, Austria
Tel: (06415) 81370 Telex: 67672
27 Rooms - Dbl from AUS 760 to 880
Open: Dec 1 - Mar 25, May 1 - Oct 25
Credit cards: DC MC VS
Swimming in small lake & skiing
Located 65 km S of Salzburg

Goldegg im Pongau is a jewel-like village nestled beside a lake and surrounded by green meadows, forests and high mountain peaks. Its graceful church spire and old stone castle rise above old wooden chalets, their windowboxes brimming with bright geraniums. This is a very unspoilt village, where the residents still go about their daily business in traditional Austrian dress, and hold to old customs. We arrived on a brilliantly sunny and crisp fall day to find the street into town blocked off due to wedding festivities. The square in front of the little white church was filled with women in colorful dirndls and men in loden suits. Tradition is also closely followed at the Gasthof Zum Bierfuhrer, a large old chalet which dates from 1480 and is chock full of antiques and "olde worlde" ambiance. The cozy wood paneled "stube" and dining room are favorites with the locals as well as with visitors. Both rooms display old paintings, antiques and other artifacts and offer a tasty, home-cooked Austrian menu. Fresh flowers and little candles warm the tables and one is tempted to linger in order to fully drink in the rustic atmosphere. The Gasthof Zum Bierfuhrer offers twelve guestrooms which all have private shower. The rooms are simple and spacious, decorated partly or entirely with painted antique furniture. Goldegg is a year-round paradise, offering miles of hiking in the summer and many trails for skiing in winter when the nearby hills take on a fairytale quality with a mantle of fresh snow.

GASTHOF ZUM BIERFUHRER
Owner: Family Burgler
Goldegg im Pongau A-5622
Austria
Tel: (06415) 8102
12 Rooms - Dbl from AUS 500 to 560
Open: All year except Nov
Credit cards: DC VS
Located 65 km S of Salzburg

The quiet simplicity and artful decor of the Schlossberg Hotel in Graz is most refreshing. After the ornate, fussy antique furniture encountered in many hotels throughout Austria, the Schlossberg Hotel is like a breath of fresh air. The mood is set by the exterior which is two simple shuttered buildings, one French blue and one pink. Inside there is a small courtyard, a tiny bar, a comfortable lounge and two very cozy breakfast rooms. The owner, Mr Marko, is a retired race-car driver. His attractive wife owns an antique store, and it is her taste for simple, predominantly country-style antiques which creates the delightful ambiance. The walls are painted white, contrasting pleasantly with the antique wooden furniture, baskets of fresh flowers and colorful old oil paintings. The bedrooms maintain the country feel, most with antique accents such as beautiful armoirs. The hotel's biggest assets are the hillside terraces reached by taking the elevator to the top floor. The view over the tiled rooftops across the river to the cathedral is spectacular. On one terrace level there is a small swimming pool. The hotel dining room serves only breakfast but there are many restaurants close by.

SCHLOSSBERG HOTEL
Owner: Family Marko
Graz A-8010, Austria
43 Rooms - Dbl from AUS 1,350 to 1,600
Open: All year
Credit cards: All major
Lovely country antiques
Small pool in terraced garden
Located in the heart of Graz

The Romantik Hotel Almtalhof is delightful - especially appealing for guests who love a country ambiance without sacrificing any of the modern amenities. Mr Leithner oversees the efficient operation of the hotel, but he told me it is his attractive wife who is responsible for the appealing decor. Hardly an inch of wall space is left unadorned - dolls, hats, miniatures, statues, wreaths, copper and etchings artistically decorate the walls. Old sleds, painted cradles, baskets of flowers, wedding chests and antique armoirs fill the rooms. To add a final "homey" touch, Mrs Leithner fills all the rooms with her lovely needlework, cross-stitching, on door plaques, pillows, tablecloths, rugs and pictures. Not to be outdone, Mr Leithner handcrafts most of the furniture - what a talented pair. The bedrooms are all nice, but request a room in the newer wing - these are larger. Room #4 is especially attractive with a beautiful large pine canopied bed, lovely paneled walls and a small sitting room overlooking the garden. Meals are served either in the cozy wood paneled dining room or else on the terrace by the river. Either place, the food is delicious - all the produce fresh from the garden and breads warm from the oven.

ROMANTIK HOTEL ALMTALHOF
Owner: Family Leithner
Grunau A-4645, Austria
Tel: (07676) 8204
23 Rooms - Dbl from AUS 900 to 1,300
Open: May 1 - Oct 15
Credit cards: DC VS
U.S. Rep: Romantik Hotels
Rep tel: 800-826-0015
Indoor swimming pool
Located 100 km W of Salzburg

Rarely have I found a more delightful small budget hotel than the Deutsches Haus am Almsee. Although tiny (only five bedrooms) and simple (none of the bedrooms has a private bathroom) the hotel is extremely charming.   Its appeal begins outside - a small chalet-style building with a high pitched roof, a balcony encircling the second floor, flowerboxes at the windows and a small outdoor patio where meals are served in the summer.   From the Deutsches Haus you look across the meadow to the shimmering green Almsee.   Inside, the attractive restaurant has heavy beamed ceilings, cheerful red draperies, an antique ceramic tiled stove and country-style wooden chairs with heart-shaped carvings.   Upstairs the bedrooms all have hot and cold water and share a bathroom down the hall. These guestrooms are cheerful, immaculately clean and cozy with down comforters plumped on the beds.   This little inn exudes a quality of caring and careful management.   The day I arrived, although everything looked spotless, the rugs were rolled up, the chairs set upon the tables, and the walls and floors were being scrubbed to a sparkling brightness.   Grete Leitner owns this small chalet-style inn and it is her style and excellent taste which make the Deutsches Haus am Almsee so appealing.

DEUTSCHES HAUS AM ALMSEE
Owner: Grete Leitner
Grunau am Almsee A-4645
Austria
Tel: (07616) 802 118
5 Rooms - Dbl AUS 340
Credit cards: None accepted
Especially nice for price
No private bathrooms
Near lovely small lake
Located 100 km W of Salzburg

Hallstatt is a very ancient village, a tiny town clinging to the steep hills which rise from the waters of the Hallstattersee. In the center of the village is a charming little square enclosed by colorful houses. Tucked into one of the corners of the square, with its flower-laden balconies just peeking into view, is the Gasthof Zauner. You enter a tiny hallway and then go up a flight of stairs to the main lobby. Probably your genial young host and chef, Mr Zauner, will be there to greet you. Up another flight of stairs are the the bedrooms. Most are rather drab and the bathrooms tiny although a few have antique decor - I would definitely ask for one of these. Do not expect too much in the way of decor in your sleeping quarters. However, the dining rooms are quite charming, especially the corner one with its mellow paneled beamed ceiling, old hunting prints and hunting trophies. The food is excellent. The inn has been in Mr Zauner's family for many generations and he has maintained the professionalism one would expect to be handed down from father to son. Grilled specialties always highlight the menu, including of course fish fresh from the Hallstattersee.

GASTHOF ZAUNER
Owner: Family Zauner
Seewirt
Hallstatt A-4830, Austria
Tel: (06134) 246
24 Rooms - Dbl AUS 500
Open: Dec - Oct
Credit cards: All major
Charming town on Hallstattersee
Located 80 km SE of Salzburg

The resort of Heiligenblut, located just south of the summit of the world famous Grossglockner Pass, is popular with tourists both winter and summer. Just north of this beautiful little town set in a hillside meadow is the Haus Senger, a chalet-style hotel whose dark wood facade has three tiers of balconies overflowing in summer with brilliant geraniums. As you walk up the hill from the parking lot, you see children playing on the swings on the front lawn while their parents sit on the terrace enjoying the sun and the stunning mountain view. A feeling of warmth and welcome permeates the air. The owners are famous for their gracious hospitality and their excellent meals. Be sure to sample their apple strudel - mit schlagg (with whipped cream) of course. Inside the hotel is quite simple with a rustic mountain decor. Some of the furnishings seemed too gaudy for my taste, but overall the ambiance is most pleasant. The bedrooms are upstairs. Many of them are suites, very practical for families. The hotel is not old, but built in the traditional chalet mountain style. What is very special here is the fabulous view and the kindness and hospitality of the owners.

HAUS SENGER
Owner: Hans & Rosy Senger
Heiligenblut A-9844, Austria
Tel: (04824) 2215
*4 Rooms and 6 Suites ***
* Dbl from AUS 580 to 860
Open: Jun - Sep and Dec - Apr
Credit cards: AX DC
Sauna, mountain view terrace
South of Grossglockner summit
Located 180 km S of Salzburg

Perched high in an unspoilt Alpine meadow above the town of Imst, the Alpenhotel Linserhof enjoys an idyllic setting. The small lake nestled in the meadow in front of the hotel invites peaceful contemplation or a quiet walk. Cared for with pride by the Linser family, the Alpenhotel Linserhof is a large structure of dark wood and white plaster built in chalet style. Charm is added by the numerous balconies overflowing with red geraniums. The restaurant is obviously a very popular dining spot, and its enclosed porch dining area affords lovely, peaceful views of the surrounding Alps. A varied menu offers traditional Austrian dishes as well as Italian specialties. A large flagstone terrace overlooking the Alpine panorama is a wonderful place to relax with an afternoon beer, the large Austrian flag flying overhead. On a cold or cloudy day, enjoy lunch or dinner in the warm, wood paneled dining room, decorated with paintings and drawings by a local artist, interspersed with numerous hunting trophies. Dramatic wrought iron accents and dark, beamed ceilings complete the typical Austrian ambiance. The 35 guest bedrooms all have private bath and are modern and functional in decor. Further guest amenities include an indoor, heated swimming pool, a library and a billiard room. This hotel is recommended primarily for its tranquil, picturesque setting and its restaurant.

ALPENHOTEL LINSERHOF
Owner: Family Linser
Imst A-6460, Austria
Tel: (05412) 2412
35 Rooms - Dbl from AUS 820
Closed: Oct 15 - Dec 15
Credit cards: AX VS
Terrace, indoor pool, sauna, solarium
Located 40 km W of Innsbruck

The Romantik Hotel Post has the ambiance of a very deluxe hotel. It is deluxe in everything but price. From the moment you walk up a flight of stairs to the main lobby, the mood is of quality and refinement: tasteful antiques abound: most of the furniture is of the formal, somewhat stiff Biedermeir period except for one cozy little dining room which is decorated in a country flavor with rustic wooden furniture and paneled walls. The formality also disappears completely as you enter onto a romantic trellised veranda which sweeps around the side of the hotel. Here lunch and snacks are served overlooking the garden, the swimming pool and the mountains. Whether served on the veranda or in the main dining room, the food is delicious. The bedrooms are pleasantly furnished - not in antiques, but in a tasteful traditional style. Although the inn looks quite new, it dates back several hundred years with many additions over the centuries, the latest being a new wing and an indoor swimming pool. There is also a large, inviting garden.

ROMANTIK HOTEL POST
Owner: Family Pfeiter
Postplatz 3
Imst A-6460, Austria
Tel: (05412) 2554
40 Rooms - Dbl from AUS 550 to 800
Open: Dec 15 through Oct
Credit cards: DC VS
U.S. Rep: Romantik Hotels
Rep tel: 800-826-0015
Swimming pool, playground
Located 50 km W of Innsbruck

Winter or summer, the Hotel-Pension Zur Linde is a delightful refuge where one can relax and be enveloped by Herr and Frau Patscheider's genuine hospitality. Their picturesque, gable-roofed and balconied house is located on a sunny corner in the small ski town of Hungerburg, 6 kilometers north of Innsbruck. In the early spring, the front terrace and garden are filled with skiiers sunning themselves, as the Zur Linde enjoys an ideal location across the street from the gondola, open year round for hikers and sightseers. Inside, the aroma of baking apple strudel welcomed us to this Tyrolean treasure trove. The house is filled with family antiques, lovely old oil paintings by local artists, and hanging wood sculptures depicting the ancient legends of this mountainous region. If asked, Frau Patscheider is happy to relate these fascinating stories to guests in her excellent English and Herr Patscheider will proudly show his magnificent collection of rare old prints and documents relating to Austria's historic hero, Andreas Hofer. The four guest bedrooms and two suites are comfortable, containing antique or pine furniture and homey touches such as paintings on the walls and a good-night chocolate on the pillow. All rooms have balconies and sink areas, but only half have private bath. In the evening, we enjoyed a delicious, traditional Austrian meal in the cozy restaurant, topped off (of course) by fresh apple strudel.

HOTEL PENSION ZUR LINDE
Owner: Family Patscheider
Innsbruck-Hungerburg A-6020
Austria
Tel: (05222) 892345
6 Rooms - Dbl from AUS 560 to 900
Credit cards: None accepted
Garden and terrace
Funicular from Innsbruck
Located 6 km N of Innsbruck

The Schloss Hotel Igls is very small, very elegant, very deluxe.   This once private mansion is conveniently located only a romantic twenty-minute tram ride from the heart of Innsbruck -   a twenty-minute ride that transports you from the busy city to a tranquil country estate.   The elegant turreted castle is set in a beautiful garden with lovely views of the mountains.   Inside the hotel has exquisite decor in both the guestrooms and the public rooms.   My favorite room is the intimate breakfast room with its French-blue walls, large windows, and cozy round tables.   On a lower level a new wing has been added with a spa, massage room and an ingenious swimming pool enclosed by walls of glass which magically disappear into the floor at a touch of a button, opening the room to the fresh air on sunny days.   In addition to the indoor-outdoor pool, there is tennis, skiing, and golf available.   Many of the converted castles lack some of the details of luxury, but such is not the case at the Schloss Hotel Igls.   This is a grand hotel suited to those who enjoy being pampered in a deluxe setting.

SCHLOSS HOTEL IGLS
Owner: Family Beck
Igls A-6080, Austria
Tel: (05222) 77217 Telex: 053314
18 Rooms - Dbl from AUS 2,540 to 3,140
Credit cards: All major
Open: Dec - Mar and May - Oct
U.S. Rep: David Mitchell
Rep tel: 800-372-1323
Golf, tennis, pool, skiing
Tram from Igls to Innsbruck
Located just S of Innsbruck

The Gasthof Zur Traube is a traditional country inn dating from 1313. Incredibly enough, the house has been in the Raitmayr family for 16 generations, and today is still a beloved family concern, managed by Hans Raitmayr, his pretty wife and his two brothers. The charm of this inn is not immediately apparent in the wide, somewhat cold, entryhall. But once through the wooden doors leading to any of the three cozy dining rooms, visitors are rewarded by the sight of low, beamed or carved wooden ceilings and warm pine paneled walls, all with a rich patina achieved only by time. Each of the dining rooms is slightly different: one has an old ceramic stove, another a collection of old pewter plates and mugs. Pretty tablecloths and fresh flowers dress the tables, and a wide variety of wines and carefully prepared dishes are offered. Upstairs, the wide hallways are a bit bare, but lead to comfortable rooms, all with private bath. The fresh, clean rooms are furnished in either contemporary knotty pine or picturesque antique painted furniture, in the Raitmayr family for generations. Most rooms have flowered balconies which look out to spectacular views of the surrounding Tyrolean scenery. A friendly gathering spot for locals and a haven for the Raitmayrs' faithful, returning clientele, the Gasthof Zur Traube is a historic, yet highly comfortable inn from which to explore the Innsbruck area.

GASTHOF ZUR TRAUBE
Owner: Family Raitmayr
Lans 9, A-6072
Austria
Tel: (05222) 77261
26 Rooms - Dbl AUS 780
Open: All year except Oct 10 - Nov 4
Credit cards: None accepted
Located 6 km S of Innsbruck

The setting of the Hotel Grunwalderhof is breathtaking - high on a plateau over-looking a beautiful green valley whose soft meadows are accentuated by a backdrop of gigantic rocky mountains.   The favorite rendezvous for guests is the grassy ter-race behind the hotel where chairs dot the green lawn - a perfect spot for soaking up the sun and the stunning view.   A path leads off to a swimming pool in the gar-den which is an oasis on warm summer days.   The view must have been the motiva-tion of the Counts of Thurn when they chose this site to build their hunting lodge. The Hotel Grunwalderhof still embraces its past.   This is not a fancy deluxe hotel, rather a comfortable "homey" lodge reflecting its hunting heritage.   There are antiques accenting all of the rooms, but the basic decor is a sporty motif with ant-lers and hunting mementos decorating the walls.   The bedrooms vary considerably in size and decor: most are quite simple although a few have some exceptionally nice antique furniture.   It is the setting that makes this hotel so very special.

HOTEL GRUNWALDERHOF
Owner: Count Franz Thurn
Patsch A-6082, Austria
Tel: (05222) 77304
27 Rooms - Dbl from AUS 560 to 1,080
Open: May - Sep 30
Credit cards: DC
U.S. Rep: Dial Austria
Rep tel: 800-221-4980
Two swimming pools, tennis
Spectacular mountain vistas
Located 8 km S of Innsbruck

The Schloss Pichlarn is a perfect choice for a "rest stop" during a tour of Austria. It would also make a good base for sightseeing because there are many sights within a short drive - the interesting town of Hallstatt, the Ice Caves, the Salt Mines, and even Salzburg are but a short drive away.   But the Schloss Pichlarn is conducive to forgetting your car for a few days and soaking in the delights of long walks along forest paths, horseback riding, tennis or golf.   In winter, skiing is the principal sport.   There is cross-country skiing from the front door or downhill on nearby ski slopes.   The hotel was formerly a privately owned castle whose origins date back to 1074.   Over the years the turreted castle has grown with many new wings and annexes, but the charm remains.   The lounges are very formal with liberal use of brocades, satins, crystal chandeliers, and Oriental rugs.   The bedrooms are also fancy in their decor, but spacious and comfortable.   Daytime is strictly informal as guests greet each other in the lobby passing by in jodhpurs, tennis shorts or golfing togs, but dinner in the beautiful dining room (decorated in shades of dusty rose) calls for tie and jacket.   The food is delicious and beautifully prepared.

SCHLOSS PICHLARN
Manager: Leonhard Rabensteiner
Gatschen 28
Irdning A-8952, Austria
Tel: (03682) 2841 Telex: 38190
77 Rooms - Dbl from AUS 2,600 to 3,600
Open: Dec 18 - Oct 31
Credit cards: AX DC VS
Golf, swimming, tennis, riding
Located 100 km SE of Salzburg

The Kurz family own and manage the Gasthof Goldener Adler and lovingly tend to the needs of their guests.   In their own words, "you and your family not only feel welcome as our guests, but as friends of the house as well."   The entire Kurz family does their best to insure that everyone is having a good time: as a result the hotel exudes a feeling of comfort and hospitality.   The hotel is on one of the main streets (just a block from a lovely, 18th-century parish church) in the small town of Ischgl. There are numerous ski-lifts in what is known as the Silvretta ski area.   Although winter is the most popular season, summer too is perfect for long mountain hikes: Mrs Kurz leads hiking excursions along beautiful trails.   The evening we were guests, the living room seemed more like a house party than a hotel as Mrs Kurz showed slides of the latest hiking adventures.   Friendliness is not all the Gasthof Goldener Adler offers.   It is an interesting historic building dating back to the 17th century.   The Kurz family has lovingly restored it, incorporating antiques into every nook and cranny - old sleds, cradles, grandfather clocks, armoirs, wedding chests and displays of antique clothing.   The bedrooms are modern in their decor, with simple new rustic wooden furniture, nice earth-tone carpets and homespun draperies.

GASTHOF GOLDENER ADLER
Owner: Family Kurz
Ischgl A-6561, Austria
Tel: (05444) 5217
30 Rooms - In Summer, Dbl from AUS 560 to 660
Open: Dec - Apr, Jun - Sep 20
Hiking and skiing
Located 130 km SW of Innsbruck

Even amoung Austria's superb selection of castle hotels, the Schloss Kapfenstein is very special.   Like most of the fortified castles, the Schloss Kapfenstein crowns the crest of a hilltop.   As you drive up the road, the woods break into open fields where grapes are planted.   These vineyards belong to the castle and yield a delicious wine.   Just before reaching the crest of the hill, you pass a beautiful tall steepled church, then round one final curve and you are at the outer gates of the castle.   You will probably be welcomed by a member of the gracious Winkler family.   Mrs Winkler, who speaks excellent English (her grandmother was from England), efficiently sees to everyone's needs.   The day we were there, she seemed to be everywhere at once - on the terrace serving glasses of wine, at the front desk managing the bills, in the kitchen overseeing the meal.   The terrace, where she was serving the guests, is spectacular: tables are set out along the walls of the castle where below you stretches a stunning panorama of rolling hills, farmland, vineyards, forests and tranquil villages.   Kapfenstein Castle is in the southeast corner of Austria so as you look to the right you see Yugoslavia and to the left Hungary. Whether served indoors or on the terrace, the kitchen prepares delicious cuisine, using only the freshest of local produce.

SCHLOSS KAPFENSTEIN
Owner: Family Winkler
Kapfenstein A-8353
Austria
Tel: (03157) 2202
*9 Rooms - Dbl AUS 800 **
* reduced rates for extended stays
Credit cards: None accepted
Closed: December to mid March
Beautiful hilltop castle
Located 60 km SE of Graz

Hotel Descriptions

The Hotel Strasshofer is located on the main street of the picturesque little town of Kitzbuhel, a colorful walled Tyrolean village dating back 700 years.   The entrance to the Hotel Strasshofer does not hold much promise - just a little street-front hallway.   It is not until you walk up a flight of stairs that you have any inkling of how nice this small hotel really is.   Arriving on the second level, you find a small lobby and two very attractive little dining rooms: one has a hunting motif with antlers decorating white walls above wooden paneling; the other has light wooden chairs and pretty gay curtains.   Another flight of stairs leads to the bedrooms.   All of the guestrooms are pleasing in decor, but some are especially appealing, decorated in what is called "bauer mobel" motif (or farmer style furniture).   These rooms cost a little more, but are really lovely with rustic-style canopied beds, light pine tables and chests, and colorful provincial print fabric used for the draperies and the slipcovered chairs and sofas.   There is a sauna in the hotel for the use of guests; however, the nicest asset of this inn is the price - very reasonable for Kitzbuhel.

HOTEL STRASSHOFER
Owner: Franz Strasshofer
Kitzbuhel A-6370, Austria
Tel: (05356) 2285
20 Rooms - Dbl from AUS 800 to 1,000
Open: Jan - Oct
Credit cards: None accepted
Sauna, skiing
Good value for Kitzbuhel
Heart of Kitzbuhel
Located 120 km SE of Innsbruck

The Hotel Zur Tenne is located in the center of Kitzbuhel. Just steps from the hotel are quaint shops filled with tempting souvenirs and gorgeous Tyrolean-style clothing, and colorful outdoor cafes serve delicious pastries. Completing the scene are brightly painted buildings, fountains, twisting little streets and ancient walls encircling the town. Although the Hotel Zur Tenne is in the village center, just a ten-minute stroll and you are in lovely mountain meadows where a wide selection of tempting paths beckon to you. The exterior of the inn is quaint - a painted facade with a terrace cafe in the front. Inside the lobby looks quite commercial, nothing special, with a large dining room located nearby. In the winter a second cozier wood paneled rustic dining room opens for the skiers. The bedrooms are especially attractive: the ambiance is country rustic with gay print draperies and handsome wooden furniture. Some of the bedrooms have beautiful four-poster canopy beds. If you want to splurge, for just a little more you can have a junior suite or apartment, which are especially attractive during winter, as they all have fireplaces. On the lower level of the hotel is a health spa with a sauna and two jacuzzis.

HOTEL ZUR TENNE
Owner: Volkhardt Falk
Vorderstadt
Kitzbuhel A-6370, Austria
Tel: (05356)4444 Telex: 5118416
46 Rooms - In summer, Dbl AUS 1,150
Open: All year
Sauna, whirlpool baths
Heart of Kitzbuhel
Located 120 km SE of Innsbruck

Romantik Hotel Tennerhof is just what one dreams of when planning a holiday to Austria, a perfect little inn - close to a picturesque village yet far enough away to feel "country", a wonderful setting in the foothills of the mountains, an inviting chalet-style exterior whose balconies in summer overflow with flowers, lovely country antiques displayed with flair, cozy bedrooms (my favorites are those in the original building), three charming dining rooms, delicious gourmet meals, indoor and outdoor pools. Plus the most important ingredient of all - wonderful hospitality. The Pasquali family own and personally oversee every detail of the hotel insuring you of a perfect holiday. The Romantik Hotel Tennerhof is definitely a hotel where you will want to linger. Relax by the pool, take leisurely walks along lovely meadow paths, hike into the mountains and explore the colorful walled village of Kitzbuhel. If you are on a winter holiday here - the skiing is superb.

ROMANTIK HOTEL TENNERHOF
Owner: Family Pasquali
Griesenauweg 26
Kitzbuhel A-6370, Austria
Tel: (05356) 3181 Telex: 51-18426
42 Rooms - Dbl from AUS 1,400 to 2,140
Open: Dec - Mar and Jun - Sep
Credit cards: DC MC VS
U.S. Rep: Romantik Hotels
Rep tel: 800-826-0015
Swimming pool, sauna, skiing
Located 120 km SE of Innsbruck

Frequently I have introduced a hotel as being a famous restaurant offering a few bedrooms. But the Romantik Hotel Musil is even more unique. Its claim to fame is a fabulous bakery - offering a few bedrooms! Dominating the corner of the hotel is a beautiful bakery with fabulous pastries which can be purchased either to take home or to eat in the adjacent cafe. The reception desk faces both the lobby and the bakery: when the shop is busy, the attendant scurries back and forth to service both sides. Passing through the lobby, you come into a circular glass-domed atrium, a bright, sunlit room where meals are served. There is also a cafe and a more formal dining room with a hunting motif. The bedrooms are large with a combination of decors: some have copies of painted furniture, others have a few antiques. The decor is nothing special but the rooms are clean and comfortable. The Romantik Hotel Musil is a good choice if you are looking for a small hotel in the heart of the old city of Klagenfurt, an especially appealing choice if you like pastries.

ROMANTIK HOTEL MUSIL
Owner: Bernd Musil
10 Oktober-Strasse 14
Klagenfurt A-9020, Austria
Tel: (04222) 511660 Telex: 42110
14 Rooms - Dbl from AUS 1,000 to 1,700
Open: All year except Christmas
Credit cards: All major
U.S. Rep: Romantik Hotels
Rep tel: 800-826-0015
Famous bakery in hotel
Located at the heart of Klagenfurt

There are no compromises in quality at the Hotel Arlberg: this is truly a deluxe hotel in every sense of the word.   You will be pampered from the moment you arrive, with excellent food served in beautiful dining rooms, tasteful antique decor in the public rooms, lovely bedrooms with excellent modern bathrooms, indoor and outdoor pools, tennis and sauna.   The nicest aspect of the Hotel Arlberg is that in spite of being a very slick operation it definitely still maintains the personality of a family-loved and operated small hotel.   The Schneider family built the hotel almost 30 years ago and it seems every year they incorporate some imaginative new improvement.   In spite of being a deluxe modern hotel it has all the warmth and charm of a small inn.   The location is also superb: the hotel snuggles in a bend of the Arlberg River which weaves through the center of Lech, one of the most picturesque ski villages in Austria.   In winter, skiing is the main attraction, with the ski tram only a short walk from the hotel.   In summer, the hotel prices drop considerably, but this is a lovely time of year to visit - there are walking paths through the mountains and meadows - a hiker's paradise.

HOTEL ARLBERG
Owner: Family Schneider
Lech A-6764, Austria
Tel: (05583) 2134 Telex: 5239122
46 Rooms - Dbl from AUS 1,200 to 2,800
Open: Nov - Apr, Jun - Sep
U.S. Rep: Steve Lohr's Ski World
Rep tel: 212-751-3250
Pool, tennis, skiing, hiking
Located a few km N of St. Anton

The Hotel Post has a prime location on the main street as you drive into the charming mountain village of Lech. It is only a short walk from the hotel to the gondola station, convenient in winter for skiing and in summer for a lift to the high mountain meadows for walking. It is not surprising the location is so superb because the Hotel Post was one of the town's first hotels. It has expanded over the years, adding many modern improvements, but the old facade is extremely inviting - a gaily painted building with green shutters and lacy stenciling decorating the plaster facade. Setting off the cheerful image in summer are red geraniums. The Hotel Post is one of the few old buildings in Lech and retains its "olde worlde" atmosphere inside with the use of wood paneling on walls and ceilings, country rustic-style furniture, pewter plates on the walls, hunting trophies, cozy fireplaces, and many pieces of antique furniture. The bedrooms vary in style but many maintain the rustic country feeling with new Alpine-style painted furniture and happy provincial print draperies. The Moosbrugger family own and operate this historic hotel that was once a post station.

HOTEL POST
Owner: Family Moosbrugger
Lech A-6764, Austria
Tel: (05583) 22060 Telex: 5239118
42 Rooms - Dbl from AUS 1,040 to 2,700
Open: Jun 28 - Oct, Dec - Apr 14
U.S. Rep: David Mitchell
Rep tel: 800-372-1323
Swimming pool, tennis, skiing
Located a few km N of St. Anton

Built in 1806, the Hotel Drei Mohren is an atmospheric old hotel with the character of a mountain fishing lodge. Photos show many happy guests with their prize-winning catches from the hotel's exclusive fishing waters in two nearby lakes and the River Loisach. Delicious fresh trout dishes can be sampled in the Drei Mohren's Tyrolean restaurant which features fine dining and tableside preparation. For dessert, twelve kinds of Austrian strudel are proudly offered. The sitting room is an inviting spot for a before or after dinner drink. It has a beamed ceiling, a small fireplace, and picture windows framed by green plants which look out to a spectacular view of the Zugspitze. In warm weather, the hotel's large outdoor terrace offers guests the same magnificent vista. The 50 bedrooms, 40 of which have private bath or shower, are simply but adequately furnished, some with antiques. All are very clean and some have pretty mountain views. Thoughtful touches such as Tyrolean designs painted around all the bedroom door frames and antique furniture and paintings in the hallways add a certain refinement to this comfortable hotel. The light and airy breakfast room is a blend of crystal chandeliers and old, gilt framed oil paintings with homey, contemporary chairs and tables. Views of the mountain scenery can be enjoyed from every table as picture windows form one side of the room.

HOTEL DREI MOHREN
Owner: Family Kunstner
Lermoos A-6631, Austria
Tel: (05673) 2362 Telex: 55558
50 Rooms - Dbl from AUS 500 to 730
Closed: Nov 15 - Dec 15
Credit cards: AX DC
Terrace, private fishing rights
About 30 km SW of Garmisch
Located 40 km NW of Innsbruck

Women especially will relate to the introduction of the history of the Hotel Traube which reads, "Each generation (since 1586) has built and improved something in order to satisfy the guests with comfortable rooms as well as a good cuisine and drinks. This achievement was basically due to the fact that the Vergeiners (the owners) got their wives and housemothers from good landlord families." Whether this successful operation is indeed due to the fact the Vergeiner men married good strong women or not, the fact remains that today the hotel is splendidly managed. When you first see the hotel you might be disappointed because the side which faces the parking area is quite modern and sterile. But once inside, the "olde worlde" ambiance quickly asserts itself with liberal use of quality antiques. As you walk through the hotel and out the opposite entrance which faces the pedestrian shopping mall, all hestitations are dispelled. This side of the hotel is charming - a rust colored building, windows trimmed in crisp white, dark green shutters, and, in front, a gay blue and white striped awning protecting a delightful outdoor cafe.

ROMANTIK HOTEL TRAUBE
Owner: Gunther Wimmer
Hauptplatz 14
Lienz A-9900, Austria
Tel: (04852)2551 Telex: 46515
*48 Rooms - Dbl from AUS 1,400 to 1,800 **
* *** Rate includes 2 meals*
Credit cards: All major
U.S. Rep: Romantik Hotels
Rep tel: 800-826-0015
Swimming pool, skiing, fishing
Located 147 km W of Klagenfurt

Burg Lockenhaus is a wonderful old castle on the top of a small mountain in the province of Burgenland, reached by a road that winds up through a densely forested hill. Just before attaining the pinnacle you go through the ancient doorway to a wonderful inner courtyard, on sunny days a hub of gaiety with wine and beer and good food being served at wooden tables. A door leads off to the right of the courtyard to a tavern-style dining room where excellent cold beer and hearty meals are served in cozy surroundings. The reception desk is in a small room close to the entrance and nearby stairs lead up to six freshly painted bedrooms, some with antique beds and beautiful views. Except for the wonderful old beds, the furnishings are not outstanding, but the views certainly are very special. (Rooms three and four are especially attractive.) There are also 29 rooms in an annex down the hill so, when making a reservation, be sure to specify a room in the castle. Some English is spoken by the staff who are gracious and helpful. The castle is also a museum so you can combine your night's stay with sightseeing.

BURG LOCKENHAUS
Owner: Family Keller
Lockenhaus A-7442, Austria
Tel: (02616) 2394
35 Rooms - Dbl from AUS 766
Open: Mar - Oct
Credit cards: None accepted
Dramatic hilltop castle
Open to public as museum
Inner courtyard cafe
Located 120 km S of Vienna

You will have no problem finding the Hotel Brau: just head toward the church steeple and look for the bright yellow hotel only a block away. The facade is exceptionally attractive, and apart from a very modern unattractive bar at the end of the lobby, the interior exudes an antique ambiance. There are two marvelous dining rooms, both cozy, but my favorite is the less formal of the two with dark wooden beams and wainscoating setting off the stark white walls which are cozily cluttered with old harnesses, guns, clusters of old cow bells hung on leather straps, horseshoes and harnesses. Against the wall there is a charming fireplace encircled by a wooden bench pierced by hearts. The same friendly hearts are repeated on the Alpine wooden country chairs. The bedrooms are pleasant, large and well furnished. The furniture is new but in a traditional style, colorfully painted. The curtains continue the country motif and gay rag rugs accent the light wooden floors. The Brau is a pleasant hotel, especially attractive from the outside, and the town of Lofer is really outstanding - a village beneath the towering Steinberge mountain range - a town so pretty its beauty is frequently captured on postcards.

HOTEL BRAU
Owner: Family Moldan
Manager: Helmuth Neunteufel
Lofer A-5090, Austria
Tel: (06588) 2070 Telex: 66535
30 Rooms - Dbl from AUS 840 to 1,340
Open: All year
Heart of village of Lofer
Very old charming inn
Surrounded by lovely mountains
Located 47 km SW of Salzburg

The Hotel Post is a picture-postcard perfect chalet style inn, whitewashed with green shutters, painted detail around the windows and wooden balconies dripping with cheerful red geraniums.   Inside, the lobby is simple but leading off to the left is a charming little dining room with mellow paneled walls, simple wooden chairs with rounded backs, comfy country print cushions and blue curtains at the windows. The bedrooms are furnished with simple wooden furniture, rag rugs on the floors and fluffy down comforters on the beds.   I was told that some of the best guest rooms have antique wooden furniture - so when making a reservation be sure to request one of these.   This is a very simple hotel - certainly nothing suitable for those seeking luxury.   But the town of Lofer is extremely attractive and the Hotel Post is a most picturesque little inn.   It is located on the main street just steps away from many beautiful small shops - many specializing in Tyrolean style clothing. The Hotel Post and the Hotel Brau (also featured in this guide are located about a block apart.   Both are charming on the outside, have appealing dining rooms and simple bedrooms.   The Hotel Post is slightly less expensive.

HOTEL POST
Owner: Helmuth Neunteufel
Lofer A-5090, Austria
Tel: (06588) 3030 or 3040
30 Rooms - Dbl from AUS 550 to 750
Open: Dec - Mar and May - Sep
Credit cards: None accepted
Beautiful old village
Surrounded by mountains
Located 48 km SW of Salzburg

The Hotel Garni Prem is a picturesque Tyrolean inn which is fastidiously looked after by the Prem family. Attired in her traditional dirndl, Rose Prem is an attractive and hospitable Austrian hostess who speaks very good English. Her family's pretty, 270-year-old chalet is found in a garden off a tiny side street in the heart of Mayrhofen. Bright red rose bushes border the lush green lawn, and fruit trees shelter the walkway to the front door. The lower windows are bordered by fresco paintings and the top two floors are ringed by light wood balconies and vari-colored geraniums. The Prem family is documented as having been in Austria since 1320, and many of their family antiques are displayed in the hotel. These painted chests and armoires, old paintings, prints and Oriental rugs add character to the public areas. The cozy wood paneled dining rooms invite guests to linger over a delicious breakfast before a day of winter skiing or summer hiking. A good night's rest is assured in the 28 functional, comfortable, and very clean bedrooms, all with private bath. All rooms also offer a romantic balcony for gazing out over the incomparable mountain scenery. In warm weather the tranquil back garden is a perfect setting for a leisurely game of cards, a good book, or quiet contemplation.

HOTEL GARNI PREM
Owner: Family Prem
Mayrhofen A-6209
Austria
Tel: (05285) 218
28 Rooms - Dbl AUS 600
Open: All year except Nov
Credit cards: None accepted
Garden
Located 70 km SE of Innsbruck

Usually a large hotel is not included in this guide, but the Millstattersee is one of the prettiest of the lakes which snuggle in the mountains of southern Austria and the town of Millstatt is one of the loveliest of the lakeside villages.   After looking at all of the lakefront hotels, the Die Forelle Hotel seems one of the very nicest.   It has a prime location out on a peninsula which curves gently into the lake. Exquisite displays of colorful flowers bloom in well-tended gardens and prettily positioned on the lawn in front of the hotel there is a small pool. A spacious terrace filled with small tables for dining overlooks the blue water and a promenade hugs the shoreline.   The hotel has two tennis courts, plus there is boating and swimming in the lake.   It is a pleasant walk to the pier from where the ferry circles the lake - always a fun excursion.   This is not a hotel just oozing with "olde worlde" ambiance, but the building dates back to the turn of the century and the lounge and dining rooms definitely have a traditional feel.   The bedrooms are modern and attractive, many with a romantic view of the lake.   They are located in two buildings which join to form this lakefront hotel.

DIE FORELLE HOTEL
Owner: Family Aniwanter
Millstatt A-9872, Austria
Tel: (04766) 2180 or 2050
42 Rooms - Dbl from AUS 1,100 to 1,880
Open: May to Oct
Directly on Millstattersee
Resort style formal hotel
Swimming pool, boating, tennis
Located 150 SE km of Salzburg

Millstatt is a colorful old town built on the slope of the hill rising from the Millstattersee, with the Hotel Post located on a small street near the main square. Most of the resort hotels which have sprung up around the lake are attractive but recently built with a modern appearance, but the Hotel Post has been a guest house for over a hundred years. The hotel, a square building whose mustard-yellow facade is accented with white trim and dark green shutters, conveniently faces the village with its array of small shops. Just a short stroll down the hill and you are at the lake front where swimming, boating, and ferry excursions are all available. The dining room is most charming with a cozy ambiance of paneled walls and ceiling, wooden tables and chairs, intricately designed wrought iron chandeliers, and fresh flowers on all the tables. The hotel has recently been enlarged and although I usually recommend the "old section" of hotels, at the Hotel Post the newer rooms are nicer: most have balconies and an attractive traditional decor. The Hotel Post has another feature rarely found in hotels - the Sichrowsky family has several children of their own and during the tourist season has a "nanny" who supervises a nursery for their children and those of their guests.

HOTEL POST
Owner: Family Sichrowsky
Millstatt A-9872
Austria
Tel: (04766) 2108
22 Rooms - Dbl from AUS 920 to 1,000
Open: All year
Former postal stop
Walking distance to lake
Located 150 SE km of Salzburg

The Alpenrose is located high above the Millstattersee with a glorious panorama of rolling hills, small farms, villages, meadows and forests - with the highlight being the beautiful Millstattersee in the distance. At first glance I thought the Hotel Alpenrose was totally new, but it was so attractive and the view from the deck so outstanding, that I decided to investigate further. I found that although most of the building is new, "olde worlde" ambiance oozes from every nook and cranny of the inside and best of all - the center of this lovely hotel incorporates a 300-year-old farmhouse, complete with darkened, heavy-beamed ceilings, a snug fireplace, and a cozy breakfast nook in a sunlit bay window. The bedrooms follow the mood set by the dining and sitting rooms, with light pine rustic furniture and provincial prints. Another bonus is the food: everything is absolutely fresh and prepared in a gourmet fashion. Truly outstanding - especially if you like the idea of healthy, hearty meals without the use of any preservatives or artificial ingredients - instead you will enjoy butter and cheeses from the farm, homemade breads, soups prepared daily and vegetables from the garden. This hotel is not inexpensive, but considering the quality of the meals included, a good buy.

ALPENROSE
Owner: Family Obweger
Obermillstatt A-9872, Austria
Tel: (04766) 2500
*32 Rooms - Dbl from AUS 1,200 to 1,600 ***
  *** Rate includes 2 meals*
Open: All year
Credit cards: None accepted
Good value for excellent meals included
Swimming pool
On hillside above lake
Located 150 SE km of Salzburg

The Hotel PLOMBERG-ESCHLBOCK is one of my favorite types of hotels - a gourmet restaurant with rooms.   What a joy to savor a feast of the finest food and wines, and then be able to push your chair from the table in contented bliss and to walk upstairs for a happy night's sleep.   Food is the star attraction at the Hotel Plomberg.   It is hard to imagine that this tiny hotel, tucked along the shore of the Mondsee, only a short drive from Salzburg, can offer what is considered by many experts to be the finest food in Austria.   The owner, Karl Eschlbock, is also the chef and his culinary creations are not only delicious, but so artistically arranged on the plate that momentarily one hesitates to destroy the beauty of the design. There are four dining rooms, each stunning.   There is also a charming little carved bar in a cozy nook with comfortable chairs, baskets of fresh flowers and an antique grandfather clock.   There are only ten guestrooms.   The rooms with a balcony have a beautiful view of the lake and the big linden tree in front of the house, but have the disadvantage of the road passing by which explains the price difference.

HOTEL PLOMBERG-ESCHLBOCK
Owner: Monika & Karl Eschlbock
Plomberg
Mondsee A-5310, Austria
Tel: (06232) 3166 or 3572
10 Rooms - Dbl from AUS 619 to 1,800
Credit cards: AX DC VS
Some of finest food in Austria
400-year-old guest house
Across the street from Mondsee
Located 33 km E of Salzburg

The Gasthof Zum Stern is one of the prettiest inns in Austria. This 18th-century inn is just oozing with "olde worlde" charm - a faded ochre facade almost entirely covered with intricate paintings, windows framed with lacy designs, gay flowers spilling from pots on windowledges, and, over the front door, a fabulous projecting six-sided oriel window beneath which flowerboxes dance with red geraniums. When you come inside you might at first be disappointed because the lobby is starkly simple, but one of the three dining rooms offers all the charm promised by the exquisite exterior: the wooden walls are mellowed dark with age, a plump ceramic stove nestles in the corner, antique pewter plates line the shelves on the walls, rustic hand-carved antique chairs surround sturdy wooden tables. The dining room in the new wing of the hotel is much more modern in mood. The food is hearty and very good - prepared from the local fresh produce and fruits. There are twelve bedrooms located on the second floor: these are fairly large and immaculately clean, but do not expect too much decor - the furnishings are very simple and the bathrooms are made of one-piece molded plastic. However, these guestrooms are most satisfactory for a budget inn - especially one with such an appealing facade and lovely dining room.

GASTHOF ZUM STERN
Owner: Josef Griesser
Kirchwege 6
Oetz A-6433
Austria
Tel: (05252) 6323
12 Rooms - Dbl AUS 380
Open: All year
Credit cards: None accepted
Beautiful 18th-century inn
Located 50 km SW of Innsbruck

Pertisau is a town which is comprised mainly of hotels, pensions and gasthofs, all built to accommodate the large number of tourists who come here to appreciate its serene setting on the edge of the Aachensee. The drive approaching Pertisau winds through pretty rolling green hills, pastures and trees complemented by many tempting picnic spots along the way. However, if you can wait, the scenery along the banks of the Aachensee is even lovelier, with dramatic views of mountains plunging right down into the lake. The Pension Enzian offers traditional Tyrolean hospitality, not fancy, but very homey. The comfortable sitting room displays hunting trophies and an antique rifle mounted above the fireplace, as well as a bookcase full of books, pewter plates and tankards. It's a cozy room for a good book in front of the fire or a chat with friends. Meals are enjoyed in the cheerful restaurant with its rose toned Alpine upholstery and matching silk flower arrangements on the tables. Friendly waitresses dressed in pretty dirndls add to the warm atmosphere. Comfort and cleanliness rather than decor are the outstanding features of the 22 bedrooms. Furnishings are modern, yet tasteful, and all rooms have private bath and balcony. This modest pension is sure to charm those travellers seeking an informal, family atmosphere.

PENSION ENZIAN
Owner: Family Niederist
Pertisau 17, A-6213
Austria
Tel: (05243) 5265
22 Rooms - Dbl AUS 560
Closed: Oct 15 through Dec 15
Credit cards: MC
Located 50 km NE of Innsbruck

The Gasthaus Zur Goldenen Ente is an atmospheric little hotel in the heart of Old Salzburg. The building dates from 1300 and is recommended for the traveler seeking atmosphere more than modern comfort. The outstanding features of this hotel are its quiet, central location and charming traditional restaurant. The entry through an old arched doorway leads into an unprepossessing hallway between the kitchen and first floor restaurant, while a tiny old stone stairway or small elevator lead up to the second floor dining room and 17 guest bedrooms. Small in their proportions and simple in their furnishings, all bedrooms nevertheless have private bath or shower. The first floor restaurant is very "old Salzburg" with dark wooden beams, old prints on the walls and pewter tankards on the high shelves. Traditional cuisine is served on tables dressed with fresh flowers and pretty tablecloths. In the morning, an Austrian breakfast buffet is served for guests. The Goldenen Ente is found on the well-known pedestrian street, the Goldgasse, and is surrounded by tiny, exclusive boutiques. This location is very picturesque and convenient for sightseeing on foot, but a bit inconvenient for parking. Guests can only bring cars close to the hotel to load and unload, and must find long-term or overnight parking on nearby streets.

GASTHAUS ZUR GOLDENEN ENTE
Owner: J. Steinwender
Goldgasse 10
Salzburg A-5052
Austria
Tel: (0662) 845622
17 Rooms - Dbl from AUS 640 to 820
Closed: Nov 1 - 15 and Feb 1 - 15
Credit cards: All major
Restaurant, elevator
Located near the center of Old Salzburg

From the moment you see the welcoming sign of the Golden Deer (Goldener Hirsch) over the front door and enter into the cozy reception hall of the Hotel Goldener Hirsch, you will be enchanted.   Everyone from the doorman in his green apron to the maid in her crisp uniform greets you warmly and wishes you a pleasant day.   Just beyond the front desk there is a central patio with a glass ceiling.   Here the friendly bartender is ready to fix you a refreshing drink.   For more substantial fare, there is a traditional restaurant in the hotel plus, just a few steps down the street, a cozy, less formal restaurant, also owned by the hotel, called the "Herzl Bratwurst" with dark rustic wood walls and heavy beamed ceilings.   It seems the hotel grew like an adolescent - in spurts.   Rooms are stuck away in all kinds of little corridors and funny little nooks.   It might take a while to remember just how to get to your room as it could involve a couple of elevators and a jumble of corridors, but once you have arrived you will be delighted.   Most of the rooms are decorated in tones of dark green and rose and combine a few antiques with more recently designed handcrafted furniture.

HOTEL GOLDENER HIRSCH
Owner: Count Johannes Walderdorff
Getreidegasse 37
Salzburg A-5020, Austria
Tel: (0662) 848511 Telex: 632967
74 Rooms - Dbl from AUS 1,900 to 4,200
Open: All year
Credit cards: All major
U.S. Rep: Robert F. Warner
Rep tel: 800-223-6625
Located in the heart of Old Salzburg

The Pension Herbert is an immaculate and charming pension located about a 15-minute walk or short ride from the center of Salzburg. Herr Herbert Lindpointner is the solicitous host who speaks excellent English. He also owns the cozy cafe next door where delicious cakes and coffees are served as well as savory lunches and dinners. The pension is a plain but attractive building which has always been a guest house since it was built in 1880. A wide wooden staircase leads upstairs to the twelve tastefully furnished bedrooms, six of which have clean and modern private baths. Painted antique chests and armoires decorate the hallways, while the bedrooms feature Bavarian style reproduction furniture. Careful attention to detail is evident in the good lighting, complementing curtains, carpets and wallpapers, and atmospheric paintings which brighten all the bedrooms. Breakfast is served in the traditional dining room on the first floor which contains heart carved wooden chairs and fresh flower posies on each table. The original pine benches built around its perimeter add to the warmth of the room. Herr Lindpointner and his Pension Herbert offer comfortable accommodation at a reasonable price, perfect for the traveler seeking a more homey atmosphere in city accommodation.

PENSION HERBERT
Owner: Herbert Lindpointner
Nonntalerhauptstrasse 87
Salzburg A-5020, Austria
Tel: (0622) 841304
12 Rooms - Dbl AUS 750
Open: All year except Feb
Credit cards: AX
Garden, parking
Located 1 km from the Mozartplatz

The Hotel Kasererbrau is an excellent choice for a reasonably priced hotel with a convenient central location in the heart of Old Salzburg (only a few minutes' walk from Mozartplatz).   You climb a few stairs from the street level to the lobby where a reception desk is located at the end of the room.   A door to the left of the lobby leads to a comfortable lounge with some antique furniture for accent.   Here the guests congregate to exchange sightseeing tips and tell of their day's adventures. The hotel is well known to Americans so you should find many English speaking guests.   The Hotel Kasererbrau is very old so naturally the bedrooms vary greatly in size and decor.   However, they are pleasantly decorated and some have wonderful antique furniture.   This hotel is very popular and, as usual, was completely full when I visited, so I was able to see only a few of the bedrooms. One had wonderful handpainted rustic style furniture and another had much more formal, but equally interesting Biedermeier furniture with beautiful wooden antique beds and chests.   Should you desire one of the superior, antique-style bedrooms, indicate your preference when making your reservation.   During July, August and September, there is a three-night minimum stay and demi-pension (breakfast and dinner) is always included in the room rate.

HOTEL KASERERBRAU
Owner: Family Giebisch
Kaigasse 33
Salzburg A-5020, Austria
Tel: (0662) 42406   Telex: 633492
30 Rooms - Dbl from AUS 1,050 to 1,700
Open: All year
Credit cards: All major
Located in the heart of Old Salzburg

The brochure of the Schloss Monchstein depicts a rather formal, somewhat severe castle, but such is not true at all.   From the moment you arrive in the lush parklike setting you are surrounded by meticulously groomed lawns and masses of brilliant flowers in well tended gardens.   The castle is actually a jumble of towers, turrets and crenelated rooflines - all softened by clinging ivy which drapes the entire castle in a garland of green.   As you go into the hotel there is a small chapel (frequently used for weddings) through the door to the left.   The lobby is entered through the main door straight ahead.   The lounges and bedrooms are in a formal decor with the liberal use of crystal chandeliers, Oriental rugs, and brocaded fabrics.   With only seventeen guestrooms the hotel seems much more like a private residence than a hotel, and indeed it was the home of the owner, Baron V. Mierka.   The Schloss Monchstein is not in the Old Town of Salzburg, but nevertheless is most conveniently located.   From the hotel it is only about a five-minute walk through a glorious forest to the lift which will whisk you to the heart of Salzburg.

SCHLOSS MONCHSTEIN
Owner: Baron V. Mierka
Monchsberg 26
Salzburg A-5020, Austria
Tel: (0662) 841363 Telex: 632080
17 Rooms - Dbl from AUS 2,000 to 3,200
Open: All year
Credit cards: All major
U.S. Rep: Dial Austria
Rep tel: 800-221-4980
Parklike setting - tennis
Located on a hill overlooking Salzburg

A stay at the Pension Nonntal is truly like visiting friends in Salzburg. Otto and Anna Heumer enthusiastically offer their personalized, very Austrian hospitality at the Pension Nonntal. Cozy guest dinners are served in the "stube", a small dining room tucked away downstairs and decorated with country rose curtains and tablecloths. The three course meals are always festive occasions where Anna serves freshly prepared regional dishes, and Otto introduces guests to a delicious variety of Austrian wines. A sumptuous morning buffet is served in the elegantly Austrian breakfast room, decorated with delicate white and gilt chairs with rose upholstery. Matching drapes frame the pretty view of the green gardens around the house. All of the guestrooms also enjoy a view of this peaceful garden. The 19 bedrooms, 2 apartments and 1 "honeymoon" suite all have private bath and are tastefully decorated and spacious. The suite is particularly atmospheric, furnished entirely in antiques. Its pretty sitting room has French doors which open onto a private terrace with a view of the Salzburg castle. The Heumers speak good English and are extremely accommodating and helpful. They will pick guests up from the airport or train station and in winter they are even known to lead guests on afternoon ski sojourns to the nearby mountains.

PENSION NONNTAL
Owner: Otto and Anna Heumer
Pfadfinderweg 6-8
Salzburg A-5020, Austria
Tel: (0662) 841427 or 846700
22 Rooms - Dbl AUS 950
Closed: Nov and Dec
Credit cards: AX MC VS
Handicapped access in two rooms
Located 1 km from the center of Salzburg

Hotel Descriptions

The Gasthof Zur Plainbrucke is a simple country inn on the outskirts of Salzburg offering low prices and traditional atmosphere. It is an inviting yellow, two-story building, its top floor windows framed by green shutters and healthy geraniums. A pretty guest garden is sheltered from the somewhat busy road by trees and is a popular dining spot in warm weather. Indoors, the typical Austrian dining room and "stube" are warmed by pine paneling and an old ceramic stove. Hunting trophies and old pewter are displayed on the walls while country print tablecloths adorn the tables. The menu is reasonably priced and offers hearty Austrian and Italian cuisine, plus special game dishes in October. The restaurant is a favorite with locals, and is thus a good spot to brush up on your German skills while enjoying a cool stein of beer. The Gasthof Zur Plainbrucke has a total of 22 bedrooms, 13 of which are located in a pretty farmhouse annex just up the road. Some rooms have antique painted furniture, but most have old style reproductions. Very friendly hosts Walter and Sophie Schweiger are understandably proud of their establishment, and happy to help guests in any way.

GASTHOF ZUR PLAINBRUCKE
Owner: Walter & Sophie Schweiger
Itzlinger Hauptstrasse 91
Salzburg A-5020
Austria
Tel: (06222) 72728 or 73883
22 Rooms - Dbl AUS 500
Closed: Dec
Credit cards: MC VS
Restaurant with garden seating
Located 3.5 km from center of Salzburg

Enter the Hotel Stadtkrug through the old arched doorway and up the long, sloped entryhall. This part of the hotel dates from 1287, and the entryway is the former horse entrance: hence the inclined floor instead of steps. It is fun to "go back in time" by imagining horses plodding up this stone hallway with its low, arched ceiling. Today guests are greeted in the wood paneled reception area by the friendly Lucian family. Locals and visitors alike frequent the cozy restaurant with its old stone arched ceilings, large lead glass window and antique accents. Forest green tablecloths are complemented by pretty print curtains and dark wood tables, chairs and benches. A traditional menu is served and prices are reasonable. Upstairs, the 25 bedrooms are a pleasant surprise for a city hotel, as they are homey and inviting with pretty print coverlets and sometimes antique painted furniture. All are very clean with private bath and phone as well as a compact little sitting area or desk. There is even a small garden in back of the hotel with tables and chairs for guests' use. The Hotel Stadtkrug is a very atmospheric, family run hotel which is really quite a bargain considering its central location and charm.

HOTEL STADTKRUG
Owner: Family Lucian
Linzer Gasse 20
Salzburg A-5020
Austria
Tel: (0662) 73545 or 79588
25 Rooms - Dbl AUS 880
Closed: Feb - Mar
Credit cards: All major
Restaurant, guest garden, elevator
Across the river from the Mozartplatz

Hotel Descriptions   159

The Gasthof Trumer Stuberl is a relatively inexpensive small hotel for the expensive city of Salzburg, but, in spite of being a bargain, it assures you of a high level of comfort in a central location.   Gracious hosts are the young, energetic couple Hermann and Marianne Hirschbichler.   They have completely updated the interior of this 600-year-old building, creating a very comfortable and tasteful city hotel.   There are only 22 guestrooms, fostering an intimate and friendly feel to the Trumer Stuberl.   Both Hermann and Marianne speak good English and are happy to help with guests' needs from laundry service to transportation for Salzburg's popular "Sound of Music" tour.   All the bedrooms have private shower and toilet, good lighting and soundproofed doors.   Furnishings are contemporary and tasteful with soft and restful colors.   Breakfast is the only meal served in the hotel, but there are many fine restaurants nearby.   The Trumer Stuberl is well located, near the center of the Old Town on a quiet side street.   Its pretty facade is brightened by pink geraniums at every window of all five stories.   A handful of foreign flags fly above the front door, welcoming visitors from all over the world.

GASTHOF TRUMER STUBERL
Owner: Marianne & Hermann Hirschbichler
Bergstrasse 6
Salzburg A-5020
Austria
Tel: (0662) 75168 or 74776
22 Rooms - Dbl AUS 920
Open: All year
Credit cards: AX
Across the river from the Mozartplatz
Near the center of Salzburg

If you have a car you might want to consider staying only about ten minutes south of Salzburg in a 17th-century country inn, the Romantik Hotel Schlosswirt. Although the hotel faces directly on to the main road, as soon as you step inside you feel a country ambiance. To the right of the lobby is an inviting dining room enhanced by country-blue tablecloths, wood planked floors, interesting old paintings on the walls, fresh flowers on the tables and pretty girls in brightly colored dirndls serving the tables. A door leads off to a second, more formal dining room. In warm weather, the favorite eating place is outside on the terrace where meals are served on tables set with brightly colored tablecloths. Whichever dining room you choose, you will not be disappointed because this small inn is probably more famous for its excellent kitchen than for its rooms. The bedrooms, though, are most attractive: like the lounges, they are tastefully decorated in a formal, traditional, early Victorian decor, many with antique wooden sleigh-style beds. Across the street there are additional rooms in an old wood and stucco farmhouse.

ROMANTIK HOTEL SCHLOSSWIRT
Owner: Family Graf
Anif bei Salzburg
Salzburg A-5081, Austria
Tel: (06246) 2175 Telex: 631169
38 Rooms - Dbl from AUS 950 to 1,400
Open: All year
Credit cards: All major
U.S. Rep: Romantik Hotels
Rep tel: 800-826-0015
Swimming in forest pool
Located 10 minutes from center of Salzburg

An appealing alternative to staying in Salzburg, especially if traveling with children, is the Schloss Haunsperg located only fifteen minutes south of Salzburg. As you approach the castle, the landscape is a bit disconcerting as the route takes you by rather dismal factories, but do not turn back, because the Schloss Haunsperg, a 14th-century castle, creates its own mood of country tranquility. As we drove in several dogs happily bounded toward us. At first I thought their joyful greeting was for us, but soon realized they had come to welcome their owner, Mrs Von Gernerth, whose car pulled in behind ours. The castle is her ancestral home and she showed us around with all the warmth and graciousness of inborn hospitality. The guestrooms are mostly mammoth suites which would be marvelous for assorted family groups. Outstanding antique furniture, beautiful Oriental carpets, lovely crystal chandeliers, fascinating old paintings, and handsome parquet floors abound in both the guestrooms and in the lounges. In spite of the magnificent antique ambiance, there is an overall feeling of faded grandeur. However, the graciousness of the Von Gernerth family quickly makes up for what might be lacking in refurbishings and you feel like a guest in a private home.

SCHLOSS HAUNSPERG
Owner: Family Von Gernerth
Oberalm bei Hallein
Salzburg A-5411, Austria
Tel: (06245) 2662
8 Rooms - Dbl from AUS 1,180 to 1,980
Open: All year
No restaurant - snacks served
Parklike setting, tennis, chapel
Located 15 minutes south of Salzburg

The Hotel Fondachhof is only about fifteen minutes from Old Salzburg by a most convenient trolley bus whose bus stop is a few minutes' walk from the hotel.   So, if you like the idea of being in a tranquil parklike atmosphere instead of staying in the city, consider the Hotel Fondachhof - a beautifully decorated, 200-year-old manor house set in its own splendid park.   The outside of the hotel is painted a mellow mustard yellow; the windows and shutters are a crisp white; the roof is of aged red tile.   The effect is a happy blend of formality softened by the lush lawns and gay flowerbeds which surround the manor.   Near the hotel, nestled in the gardens, is a heated pool.   Joggers will be delighted to see an inviting gravel path winding across the lawn and for long jaunts extending further afield through a garden gate. Within the house the guestrooms are decorated with sedate antiques.   Some of the bedrooms are located in the original manor house while others are in an annex in the garden.   There is a charming small dining room which is for the exclusive use of the hotel guests.

HOTEL FONDACHHOF
Owner: Dr Kurt Asamer
Gaisbergstrasse 46
Salzburg-Parsch A-5020, Austria
Tel: (0662) 20906 Telex: 632519
30 Rooms - Dbl from AUS 1,650 to 2,600
Open: All year
Credit cards: AX DC MC VS
U.S. Rep: Dial Austria
Rep tel: 800-221-4980
Lovely park setting with pool
Located ten minutes by trolley from Salzburg

Klessheim Castle, located about ten minutes by car from downtown Salzburg, is a gorgeous showplace, originally owned by the brother of Emperor Franz Josef I. The front "lawn" is a splendid estate of manicured gardens with clipped hedges, large shade trees, beautiful fountains, and colorful beds of flowers.   Unfortunately, unless you are of noble birth, you will probably never be invited to the castle which is now owned by the government and used as a "guest house" for visiting royalty. However, you can easily "pretend" at the Schlosshotel Klessheim which, while not as elegant, faces onto the same superb park and is enclosed within the same stately gates.   From the terrace French doors open into a splendid central lounge with enormous crystal chandeliers, glowing hardwood floors, Oriental carpets and ornate furniture.   In the garden there are a swimming pool and tennis courts. There is, on the palace grounds, a nine hole golf course that can be used by prior arrangement if the guest is a member of another golf club.   The hotel is open only in July and August but if your holiday in Austria happily coincides with that time of year, you can live like a king only a few kilometers from Salzburg.

SCHLOSSHOTEL KLESSHEIM
Manager: Harald Neumayr
Siezenheim
Salzburg A-5071, Austria
Tel: (0662) 850877
23 Rooms - Dbl from AUS 1,020 to 2,360
Open: July and August
Credit cards: AX DC
Tennis, pool, golf available
Set in a beautiful park
Located a ten-minute drive from Salzburg

Scharding is a postcard-pretty little town, looking more like a painted backdrop for an operetta than a "real" town. A fountain graces the central square which is encircled with gaily painted, narrow buildings whose roof lines step up in a wonderful assortment of shapes and designs. The effect is one of gaiety and charm. Every exceptionally pretty hamlet needs a good hotel and luckily Scharding has the Forstingers Wirtshaus, located half a block from the square. The facade is very old and quite simple: it is a boxy green building with an arched doorway. But within you are greeted with warmth, both from the cozy decor and from the owners. The attractive young Mrs Forstinger will probably be at the front desk to greet you - her blond hair drawn back in a bun and wearing an Austrian dirndl. If you are not staying the night, you might still want to stop for a meal in one of the series of dining rooms which stretch the length of the building. These are all attractive, one having an interesting collection of antique fishing gear (Scharding is famous for its fishing). The bedrooms are decorated in a variety of styles: some are quite modern in their decor; a couple have beautiful antique painted furniture. But my favorites were the rooms with new light pine furniture and traditional rustic style four-poster beds.

FORSTINGERS WIRTSHAUS
Owner: Family Forstinger
Unterer Stadtplatz 3
Scharding am Inn A-4780, Austria
Tel: (07712) 2302
20 Rooms - Dbl AUS 640
Open: All year
Credit cards: None accepted
Medieval town with painted houses
Near German border
Located 103 km N of Salzburg

Although the building dates back to 1618, the Romantik Hotel Alte Post derives its name from 1808 when the building was reconstructed for use as a postal stop. Today the hotel has all the modern amenities, but the traditional atmosphere remains with vaulted ceilings and cozy paneled dining nooks. The entry reception room is not overly attractive, a bit too gaudy for my taste, with a brightly painted reception desk and a large-print carpeting, but once beyond the lobby, the rooms greatly improve in their "olde worlde" ambiance. There are many small dining rooms oozing with charm which are tucked into various nooks and crannies of the first floor - my favorite being a small one paneled in mellowed dark oak. Although the bedrooms all have new furniture they are especially appealing, with traditional, rustic style wooden furniture and bright provincial print draperies and cushions. But it is the food which is the hotel's most outstanding feature. The hotel is a member of the "Chaine de Rotisseurs" - the gourmet association whose name alone implies excellence of cuisine. Another plus for the hotel is the owners, the Huber family, who personally oversee each detail of the hotel to insure your stay is a happy one.

ROMANTIK HOTEL ALTE POST
Owner: Family Huber
Hauptplatz 10
Schladming A-8970, Austria
Tel: (03687) 22571 Telex: 38282
34 Rooms - Dbl from AUS 860 to 1,180
Open: Dec - Oct
Credit cards: AX DC MC
U.S. Rep: Romantik Hotels
Rep tel: 800-826-0015
Located SE of Salzburg

The Hotel Krone's greatest fame is as a restaurant, and indeed there is a stunning restaurant with a decor so charming that you would love it even if the food were not outstanding - which it is.   The room is completely enclosed in warmly hued wood - hardwood floors, intricate paneled walls, and a beautifully detailed ceiling.   The windows, deeply set within the thick walls, are of bottle glass, accentuated by country print draperies.   Around the wooden tables are beautifully carved rustic Alpine chairs.   Cowbells, antique copper, old prints, Oriental rugs, and fresh flowers complete the picture of perfection.   In summertime there is a terrace, adjacent to the inn, where meals are served beneath gay umbrellas.   Although food is the principal attraction at the Hotel Krone, you might well want to consider staying for a few nights enjoying the picturesque village of Schruns.   This is an especially attractive old village of many colorful buildings with a river rushing through the center.   In winter the town is famous for skiing, in summer for hiking.   If you want to linger, the Hotel Krone has some very reasonably priced bedrooms.   They all vary in decor and many are exceptionally attractive with beautiful antique beds.   The owner, Mr Mayer, personally oversees this small hotel.   He is most gracious and speaks excellent English.

HOTEL KRONE
Owner: Robert Mayer
Schruns-Montafon A-6780, Austria
Tel: (05556) 2255
9 Rooms - Dbl from AUS 560 to 760
Credit cards: None accepted
Wonderful old mountain village
Summer hiking, winter ski resort
Located in SW Austria - 13 km S of Bludenz

The Hotel Hirschen has one of the most beautiful dining rooms in Austria - French blue curtains contrasted against mellow wooden paneled walls, low ceilings with intricate pine paneling, blue tablecloths harmonizing with the blue draperies, sheer curtains trimmed in handmade lace, fresh flowers on the tables, rustic wooden carved chairs and an old ceramic stove in the corner.   In addition to my favorite dining room, the Hotel Hirschen has four others each delightful and each different.   Doing the decor justice, the food is delicious: some of the best we had in Austria.   This small hotel is efficiently and warmly managed by Franz Fetz whose family has owned the Hotel Hirschen for many generations.   The emphasis of this small inn (dating from 1757) is the gourmet kitchen; however, Mr Fetz also provides some excellent accommodations.   There is a new wing with small modern rooms in light wood.   But splurge and ask for the antique-style rooms in the original section. They are much more attractive and the view over the small village square to the old church is charming.

HOTEL HIRSCHEN
Owner: Franz Fetz
Hof 14
Schwarzenberg A-6867, Austria
Tel: (05512) 2944 Telex: 59573
12 Rooms - Dbl from AUS 830 to 1,170
Closed: Apr 15 - 30, Nov - mid Dec
Credit cards: MC DC
Beautiful old country inn
Located in NW Austria

St. Wolfgang in the summer is the target for busloads of tourists from Salzburg who want a taste of the beautiful Austrian Lake District.   In the heart of this colorful village, perfectly positioned on the lake front, is the Hotel Im Weissen Rossl. Although the hotel has been refurbished in a style that unfortunately has destroyed much of its "olde worlde" charm, the location cannot be surpassed.   By midday the town of St. Wolfgang is congested with tourists from Salzburg, but when evening comes and the last of the buses head for home, the small village reveals its enchantment as the lake shades into golden hues with the setting sun.   To capture the view, when making reservations ask for a room overlooking the lake.   If you are unable to secure a lake view room, do not despair, you can admire the lake from the dining terrace on the lakeshore.   The Peter family, owners of the hotel for three generations, have thoughtfully provided areas of the hotel exclusively for the use of the guests so as to protect them from the influx of hoards of daytime visitors. The Weissen Rossl used to be open only in the summer months, but in recent years the inn greets guests also in winter when the village is especially beautiful and less crowded.

HOTEL IM WEISSEN ROSSL
Owner: Family Peter
St. Wolfgang A-5360, Austria
Tel: (06138) 2306 Telex: 68148
68 Rooms - Dbl from AUS 760 to 1,420
Open: Dec 21 - Nov 11
Credit cards: All major
U.S. Rep: Romantik Hotels
Rep tel: 800-826-0015
Beautifully situated on St.Wolfgangsee
Tennis, water sports, ferry dock
Located 50 km E of Salzburg

The Schloss Ernegg, a wonderful old castle encircled by a 500-acre estate, is owned by the gracious Countess Auersperg. She mentioned to me in a letter that although the castle dates from the 11th century, it has ONLY been in her family since 1675. The Countess's father was killed in World War II and the family transformed their home into a small hotel. However, according to the Countess, "we never like to call it a hotel; our twenty bedrooms all have names and we still try to run it very much more like a private house with paying guests than a hotel", and that is exactly the mood achieved. Consequently this small castle hotel will not be for everyone: there is no "slick" hotel ambiance and the bedrooms, although most enormous and containing excellent antiques, show the strain of time and a low budget. The lounges abound with priceless family heirlooms although a faded elegance prevails. However, for those who enjoy the intimacy of being a guest in a spectacular castle with a hostess and staff whose warmth and friendliness enhance your stay into the mood of a house party among friends, this will be a very special experience. Note for train buffs: the hotel is very close to the Steinakirchen narrow gauge railway station.

SCHLOSS ERNEGG
Owner: Countess Maria Auersperg
Steinakirchen A-3261, Austria
Tel: (07488) 214 Telex: 19289
20 Rooms - Dbl from AUS 690 to 970
Open: May 1 - Oct
Credit cards: MC VS
Riding, fishing, 9-hole golf course
11th-century castle - forest setting
Located 120 km W of Vienna

Steyr is an exceptionally charming old town whose central plaza is lined with rainbow-hued medieval houses, most of them tall and narrow with colorful red-tiled roofs. Perfectly located, facing the main plaza in the heart of the old town, are two especially attractive three-story houses joined together with a series of suspended arches. Originally each house was a separate hotel - one called the "Inn to the Three Allies" and the other the "Inn of the Three Roses". Several years ago both hotels were renovated and cleverly joined together to form the Hotel Mader. Not that the hotel business is a new venture - for 300 years inns have occupied the two small houses. The recent renovation has produced an excellent modern hotel with each bedroom having its own private bath and direct dial telephone. Although the bedrooms are modern in decor, they are very attractive with nice wooden furniture, white walls, colorful print draperies, and crisp white curtains. There are two restaurants which, like the lobby and lounges, have some antique accents. One of the most appealing and unusual parts of the hotel is the inner courtyard - surrounded by arcaded walkways - where meals are served in the summer.

HOTEL MADER
Owner: Family Mader
Stadtplatz 36
Steyr A-4400, Austria
Tel: (07252) 23350 Telex: 28302
55 Rooms - Dbl from AUS 650 to 840
Open: All year
Credit cards: MC VS
U.S. Rep: Traute Lyon
Rep tel: 301-838-1161
Located 40 km S of Linz

The Hotel Krone has all the right ingredients for a country inn - small, very old, with a beautiful facade, lovely antiques, good cooking, attractive bedrooms, large modern bathrooms, and, best of all, gracious owners who speak English. The combination is very hard to find, especially in inexpensive small inns in secluded valleys. The Hotel Krone is immediately appealing, a square box of a building ornamented in the corner with a fabulous multi-faceted bay window intricately decorated with bright colorful designs. There are shutters at some of the windows while others are outlined with painted designs. A whimsical gold sign dangles above the street suspended from a wrought iron brace. Outside tables are set for dining. Inside are several dining rooms, each a jewel of antique woods and provincial print curtains. On the second floor is a museum-quality room dating back to the 17th century now used just "for show". The third floor contains six nice bedrooms, not with antique furniture, but lovingly decorated by Mrs Marberger, some with painted furniture, others with classic wood furniture. Mr and Mrs Marberger recently took over the management of the hotel when his father retired. I asked the charming Mrs Marberger if the inn had been in her husband's family a long time. "No", she said, "only about 200 years."

HOTEL KRONE
Owner: Family Marberger
Umhausen A-6441, Austria
Tel: (05255) 5212 or 5202
6 Rooms - Dbl from AUS 400 to 600
Closed: Apr
Credit cards: None accepted
Excellent value, lovely inn
Located 60 km SW of Innsbruck

Our stay here was a very special one, high-lighted by an imaginative and delicious six-course gourmet dinner in the Altwienerhof's authentic old Viennese "Winter Garden". Popularized at the turn of the century in wealthy Vienna townhomes, the "Winter Garden" is a glassed-in room which looks out into a walled garden. In the summer, guests are treated to a view of a flower-filled bower, while in the winter the garden becomes a fairytale landscape as snowflakes drift down in the soft light of gas lamps. The room is fresh and inviting, filled with an assortment of plants and flowers among the white wrought iron chairs and tables. Gleaming silver, china and glassware complete the picture of this unusual "garden". Guests may also dine in the atmospheric, cherry paneled dining room, which offers subdued candlelight and an elegant ambiance of a bygone era. It is important to note that the budget prices of the rooms are not reflected in the restaurant prices: some of the finest cuisine and wine available in Vienna are offered here and are priced accordingly. Rudolf Kellner is the head chef, and he and his wife Ursula are very proud of the fact that the Altwienerhof has recently been classified as one of the twenty best restaurants in the entire country of Austria. The bedrooms at the Altwienerhof vary from large, impeccably furnished suites to simple, modern bedrooms which share a bath.

ALTWIENERHOF
Owner: Rudolf & Ursula Kellner
Herklotzgasse 6
Vienna A-1150, Austria
Tel: (0222) 837145
23 Rooms - Dbl from AUS 760 to 925
Open: All year
Credit cards: AX
Restaurant, garden, elevator
Located near the Schonbrunn Palace

This atmospheric pension began as a small, luxury hotel in 1913. Although it is now considerably scaled down in size, one can easily imagine its former grandeur from the abundance of fine antiques still in evidence. Entering the Pension Franz is like discovering a lovely pearl inside an oyster shell as the building is very unprepossessing from the outside. In addition, one must pass through a rather drab entry and climb a flight of stairs before being rewarded by the sight of the rich cherrywood paneling and fine antiques in the guest lounge and reception area. It is a great temptation to just sit and rest in the warm red tapestry chairs, under the pretty brass chandelier which lights up the wood beamed ceiling. A lace covered table with a bouquet of fresh flowers complete this charming room. All of the 24 bedrooms have bath or shower, but not all have a private toilet. The rooms are prettily furnished with white and gilt reproductions, old oil paintings, vases and Oriental rugs. Some traffic noise might be heard from the front rooms, but the views of the Gothic cathedral across the street and the ornate town hall a block or so away are a wonderful sight for visitors to Vienna. We were surprised by the intimate, yet elegant, breakfast room that greeted us the morning of our stay. A lovely little stained and leaded glass window let in morning light as we took our places at a lace covered table. Large oil paintings of the 1800s and oversize antique vases set a mood of days gone by.

HOTEL PENSION FRANZ
Hotelier: Alice Gesmbh
Wahringerstrasse 12
Vienna A-1090, Austria
Tel: (0222) 343638 or 343639
24 Rooms - Dbl from AUS 890 to 990
Open: All year
Credit cards: AX DC VS
Located 3 blocks N of the town hall

The Hotel im Palais Schwarzenberg is expensive, but unique. Although only about a ten-minute walk to the heart of Vienna, you feel you are staying in the country. You can live like royalty in a splendid ornate 17th-century palace surrounded by over 18 acres of exquisite gardens, where paths lead past manicured flower beds, arches of beech trees, fountains and statues. The mood is intimate, with a small reception lobby, elegant antique-filled waiting room, beautiful bright tea room, a formal dining room, plus a glass-enclosed dining terrace. The decor is consistently tasteful with excellent antique furniture, valuable original art and masses of fresh flowers. The new wing is attractively furnished with sedate decorator-coordinated fabrics. These rooms overlook the parking courtyard but are very quiet. Only about 10 of the rooms overlook the gardens - all the ones I saw were outstanding, with beautiful antiques. These rooms are the more expensive ones and since there are so few, they cannot be guaranteed in the busy season. The old section of the Palais Schwarzenberg (used mostly for private functions or concerts) is museum-like in its beauty with many priceless objects of art, including two Reubens paintings.

HOTEL IM PALAIS SCHWARZENBERG
Owner: Prince Von Schwarzenberg
Schwarzenberg-Platz 9
Vienna A-1030, Austria
Tel: (0222) 784515 Telex: 136124
42 Rooms - Dbl from AUS 3,000 to 4,500
Open: All year
Credit cards: All major
U.S. Rep: Preferred Hotels
Rep tel: 800-323-7500
Located in a park in Vienna

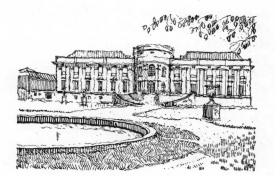

The location of the Romantik Hotel Romischer Kaiser could not be more perfect - only a few minutes' walk to the Opera and just steps from the splendid pedestrian shopping street, the Karntner Strasse.   Even though in the heart of old Vienna, the hotel faces a small side street, thus avoiding some of the noise and confusion of the city.   In front of the hotel there is a small terrace where guests can sit to relax after shopping or sightseeing.   Entering the hotel, you find a small, pleasant reception lobby decorated with a crystal chandelier, Oriental carpets, and fancy chairs upholstered in needlepoint.   A tiny, slightly stuffy lounge is to your right and a little breakfast room to your left.   Although the furnishings seem a bit stiff and formal, the management is most warm and gracious.   The Jungreuthmayer family owns the hotel and happily oversee the mangement, insuring your stay will be a most pleasant one.   There are 27 bedrooms: some are quite elaborate with ornate gilt furniture; others are more modern in their decor.   None of the guestrooms are outstanding, but they are pleasant and a good value for Vienna.   Buffet breakfast is the only meal served, but many excellent restaurants are just steps away.

ROMANTIK HOTEL ROMISCHER KAISER
Owner: Family Jungreuthmayer
Annagasse 6
Vienna A-1010, Austria
Tel: (0222) 5127751 Telex: 113696
27 Rooms - Dbl from AUS 1,500 to 1,960
Open: All year
Credit cards: AX DC MC VS
U.S. Rep: Ray Morrow Associates
Rep tel: 800-243-9420
Located in the center of Vienna

For opera lovers or shopping enthusiasts, there is no hotel more perfectly situated than the Hotel Sacher. It is located across the street from the world famous Vienna Opera House and steps from the most famous shopping street in Vienna, the Karntner Strasse. Although the Hotel Sacher, with 124 rooms, is larger than most hotels included in this guide, it would be remiss of us to leave out a hotel which has been an integral part of Vienna's history for so many years. Since 1876 the Hotel Sacher has been the gathering place for royalty, artists, politicians, opera singers, actors, and the beautiful people of Vienna. Step into the small corridor off the lounge to enjoy some of the nostalgic photographs of the Hotel Sacher's more famous guests. But it is not only sentimentalism and location which make the Hotel Sacher so appealing: the rooms exude a romantic "olde worlde" charm - from the glass ceilinged, wood paneled lounge whose Oriental carpets, heavy chandeliers, and antique furniture beautifully reflect the past, to the bar with red brocaded walls and crystal chandeliers. There are several restaurants - especially popular is the elegant coffee house which still serves the delicious rich chocolate cake with the apricot filling which has become famous the world over - the Sacher torte of course.

HOTEL SACHER
Philharmonikerstrasse 4
Vienna A-1015, Austria
Tel: (0222) 51456 Telex: 112520
123 Rooms - Dbl from AUS 2,100 to 3,400
Open: All year
Credit cards: All major
Located in the heart of Vienna

The Hotel Zur Wiener Staatsoper offers reasonably priced rooms and a wonderfully old-fashioned atmosphere right in the heart of Vienna. The pretty, white baroque facade welcomes guests with a selection of international flags flying over the front door. A filagree wrought iron door leads into the gilt and crystal lobby area where your host, Walter Ungersbock, extends his greeting. The Hotel Zur Wiener Staatsoper is located on a pedestrian street, thus quiet prevails in the high ceilinged guestrooms. Delicate flower print wallpapers, matching curtains, crystal chandeliers, and reproduction white furniture create a fresh, feminine feeling in the rooms. All rooms have a private shower, W.C. and telephone. There is no restaurant at the Zur Wiener Staatsoper, but a satisfying Continental breakfast is served. The breakfast room is pretty and inviting, with rose toned tapestry chairs and old prints on the walls. Take advantage of the marvelous location of the Zur Wiener Staatsoper and go on foot to visit the many nearby coffeehouses and tempting shops along the Kartnerstrasse. The hotel offers no parking, but spots can usually be found without too much difficulty on neighboring streets.

HOTEL ZUR WIENER STAATSOPER
Owner: Walter Ungersbock
Krugerstrasse 11
Vienna A-1010
Austria
Tel: (0222) 5131274
22 Rooms - Dbl AUS 850
Open: All year
Credit cards: None accepted
Close to the Opera House
Located near the Kartnerstrasse

You will not have any trouble finding the Romantik Hotel Post. Just look for the tall church spires in the middle of Villach, wind your way to the heart of the Old Town, where you will find on the same street, a few steps away from the church, your goal - the Romantik Hotel Post. The hotel is very old. Records dating to the 16th century show it as a palace belonging to the Counts of Khevenhuller. It is not known exactly when it was converted into a hotel, but from the 18th century the Hotel Post begins to appear in official documents as an inn. Since that time it has been host to many famous persons including the Empress Maria Theresa. Today the hotel restaurant reflects its history as a postal stop: it has a charming "mail coach motif" with fascinating antique prints of old mail coaches artfully arranged on the walls. In addition to the mail coach room, there are several other very attractive dining rooms - one with a hunting motif with trophies displayed on the walls. In the rear there is a small courtyard where snacks are served when the weather is warm. The bedrooms vary considerably: some are a bit drab whereas others are quite attractively decorated in antiques. I suggest splurging and requesting one of the best rooms.

ROMANTIK HOTEL POST
Owner: Dr F. Kreibich
Hauptplatz 26
Villach A-9500, Austria
Tel: (04242) 26101 Telex: 45723
68 Rooms - Dbl from AUS 860 to 1,100
Open: All year
Credit cards: AX DC MC
U.S. Rep: Romantik Hotels
Rep tel: 800-826-0015
Near the border of Yugoslavia & Italy
Located in the south of Austria

The setting of the Jagdschloss Graf Recke is delightful, situated in a meadow just above the town of Wald im Pinzgau.   The outstanding feature of this hotel is not its lovely mountain location but the warmth and character which permeates this old hunting lodge.   Do not expect luxurious accommodations: this inn is exactly what it is supposed to be, the family hunting lodge of the noble Count Recke Family. Here you can sink into the past and feel you are at a house party, an invited guest on one of the Count's hunting expeditions.   As Count Recke explained to me, his father and grandfather would arrive from their castle in Poland to hunt (their private hunting grounds is now a National Park): at the end of the day, the hunters eagerly returned to the lodge anticipating the camaraderie of a drink in the cozy bar, a delicious well-cooked dinner, and a clean comfortable bed.   This is exactly what you too can still expect - nothing fancy but a special experience.   A real home atmosphere, delicious food, comfortable beds, and the warmth and graciousness of the kind Recke family.   This comfortable old hunting lodge is an excellent choice for a holiday.

JAGDSCHLOSS GRAF RECKE
Owner: Count Recke
Wald im Oberpinzgau A-5742, Austria
Tel: (06565) 6417 Telex: 66711
24 Rooms - Dbl from AUS 900 to 980
Credit cards: DC VS
U.S. Rep: Dial Austria
Rep tel: 800-221-4980
Swimming pool, hiking, hunting
Old hunting lodge, lovely setting
Located 75 km SE of Innsbruck

The Hotel Schoneben is truly a perfect example of an Austrian country inn, inside and out. Perched on a grassy hillside amidst spectacular mountain scenery, it is made up of two white plaster chalets, accented by dark wood balconies overflowing with bright geraniums. Inside, one finds a Tyrolean treasure chest of antiques, warm wood paneling, beamed ceilings and fresh flowers. It is as if the German term "gemutlichkeit" were invented to describe this inn. Pretty Alpine print fabrics adorn the dining room windows and bench upholstery, while carved wooden chairs and tables grace the warm tile floors. Dinner on the terrace or in the cozy dining rooms is a romantic treat. A rustic elegance pervades this inn, whose oldest part dates from 1604. Host Stefan Schneider offers 17 lovely bedrooms and 4 apartments, all with private bath and phone. Most of the rooms and all the apartments have either a balcony or a garden terrace, and all are filled with carved pine furniture. Special touches such as fresh flowers, lace curtains, and old framed prints add warmth and charm. The apartments are newer, but care has been taken to maintain the hotel's rustic flavor with beamed ceilings, pine furnishings and soft colors. A visit here is a memorable experience, as Stefan Schneider's great love of Austria, her culture and people is expressed in every detail of the Hotel Schoneben.

HOTEL SCHONEBEN
Owner: Stefan Schneider
Wald im Pinzgau A-5742, Austria
Tel: (06565) 82890
21 Rooms - Dbl AUS 640
Open: All year except Nov
Credit cards: None accepted
Restaurant, cafe
Located 75 km SE of Innsbruck

The Raffelsbergerhof is an especially attractive hotel located just a short stroll from the River Danube in the heart of the Wachau wine district of Austria. The hotel was originally the home of the controller of the river traffic: it must have been a lucrative job because his home is outstanding. The outside is extremely appealing - looking much more like a French manor house than an Austrian inn. The hotel is two mansard roofed buildings joined by a two-story walkway punctuated with a series of arches. You enter through heavy wooden doors into an inner courtyard formed by the two sections. The staircase to the right leads to private living quarters and the staircase to the left leads up to the second floor where the hotel reception desk is located. When I visited the hotel the reception was extremely gracious and the hotel was immaculate and attractive with antique chests, old sleds, wrought iron light fixtures and fresh flowers providing an inviting atmosphere. The bedrooms are spacious, clean and attractive although their furnishings are modern rather than antique. On the outside of the hotel an enormous grapevine is cleverly espaliered across the length of the building - a most appropriate decoration for a wine village inn.

RAFFELSBERGERHOF
Owner: Hubert Anton
Weissenkirchen A-3610
Austria
Tel: (02715) 2201
12 Rooms - Dbl from AUS 650 to 900
Open: May 1 - Oct 31
Credit cards: MC
Lovely 16th-century manor
Near the dock for ferry
Located on Danube 96 km W of Vienna

The Sporthotel Alpenhof had won my heart and a place in this guide before I had even arrived in Austria.   How could I possibly resist a hotel which gives you a key to your very own chicken box?   The key unlocks what looks like a post-office box in the henhouse and every morning your chicken - whether it be Claudia, Susie, Monika, Olga or one of their sisters - will be sitting there protecting your very own fresh egg.   In the morning each guest strolls out to the chicken coop, finds the box with his chicken's name on the door, collects his egg, and then returns to the terrace for an exquisite breakfast buffet - a feast of fresh cheeses, farm butter, homemade jams, piping hot breads, country ham, fresh orange juice - plus, of course, your egg cooked to your special taste.   The chicken story is just an indication of the incredible love, caring, professionalism, and even humor with which the Zohrer family orchestrates the Sporthotel Alpenhof.   The hotel is nestled in a beautiful meadow which gently slopes down to the shimmering green Weissensee.

Hotel Descriptions

The views from the terrace and many of the bedrooms are gorgeous: the lake stretches out before you, framed by forests which rise steeply from the shore. To the east the lake narrows and the hills rise more precipitously to give a fjord-like beauty. Around the lake are perfect hiking paths and there is even a lazy steamer that glides across the waters to pick you up from strategically placed piers and bring you "home" again should you weary. The rooms at the Sporthotel Alphenhof vary tremendously. Many are family suites with special little nooks for the children, others have new wooden furniture painted with an Alpine motif, one is "Grandfather's Bedroom", furnished with his original wooden Victorian style furniture. None of the bedrooms are "cutesy pretty" but all are outstanding in their comfort. This 300-year-old farmhouse has blossomed into a traditional yet modern hotel. The food is fabulous - with 180 acres of farmland the food is all homegrown and scrumptious. You can choose from gourmet delights or special diet meals. But do not expect to "drop in" during season: the hotel is fully booked months in advance.

SPORTHOTEL ALPENHOF
Owner: Family Zohrer
Naggl 4
Weissensee A-9762, Austria
Tel: (04713) 2107 Telex: 48267
28 Rooms - Dbl from AUS 1,220 to 2,010
Open: May - Oct, Dec - Easter
Credit cards: None accepted
Wonderful old farmstyle inn
Located in southern Austria

Gralhof Pension, a delightful small inn, is located across the road from the emerald green Weissensee. It has its own grassy lawn stretching down to the lake where a wooden pier is available for swimming, boating or fishing. The hotel is a farmhouse dating back 500 years - one of the oldest farmhouses in the valley. The lower part of the building is of white stucco and the upper portion constructed of wood. Wooden balconies with carved banisters and windowboxes overflowing with red geraniums encircle the inn. The inside is immaculate. Most of the light pine furniture is new but there are accents such as an antique cradle, antlers, deer skins, wedding chests, red checked curtains and family portraits giving a country flavor. The food is country-simple and delicious. Mrs Knaller, who is young and gracious, and speaks English very well, was cooking dinner when we arrived. The smells from the kitchen were enticing and she explained that her husband is a farmer and all the milk, butter, cheeses and vegetables are fresh. Before dinner you might want to take a short walk down the road and board one of the ferries which circle the lake.

GRALHOF PENSION
Owner: Family Knaller
Neusach
Weissensee A-9762, Austria
Tel: (04713) 2213
*18 Rooms - Dbl AUS 720 to 820 **
*   * Price includes breakfast and dinner*
Credit cards: All major
Closed: mid Oct - mid Dec, end Mar - end Apr
Exceptionally nice budget hotel
500-year-old farmhouse
Boating and swimming in the lake
Located 170 km S of Salzburg

The Schloss Leonstein is located on the busy main street of the small lake resort town of Portschach. However, once you have entered into the grounds, you are isolated from the hustle and bustle of the town. The grounds are lovely: not only is this old castle surrounded by lawns, but flower gardens are tucked into the small courtyards where large trees, walkways, green grass and ivory colored walls please the eye. In the summer, chamber music concerts are frequently given in the courtyard. The reception area is light and airy with lovely antiques, contrasting with the somewhat dark and stuffy lounges. The dining room is very attractive, with vaulted ceilings, Oriental carpets and high-backed upholstered chairs. Most important, the food is rated among the best in Austria. Although the hotel is across the street from the lake, it has its own private lakeside park where towels, lockers, lounge chairs and small boats are available for the guests. It is also an easy walk down to the pier where you can board one of the ferries which circle the lake.

SCHLOSS LEONSTEIN
Owner: Aldo Neuscheller
Portschach
Worthersee A-9210, Austria
Tel: (04272) 28160 Telex: 0422019
30 Rooms - Dbl from AUS 1,360 to 2,320
Open: mid May - end Sep
Credit cards: AX DC VS
Weekly concerts in summer
Boating & swimming in lake
Tennis and lakeside garden
Located in southern Austria

The Schloss Seefels, built in 1860 as a private estate, makes a wonderful stopover on a busy itinerary. Here you can relax and be pampered for a few days while soaking in the beauty of the Worthersee. A grassy lawn goes from the hotel to the lake where a wooden pier stretches over the water for sun-bathing and swimming. Boats are docked for water sports with an attendant to assist with boat excursions, water-skiing or wind-surfing. An indoor pool extends from within the hotel outside onto the lawn, thus accommodating swimmers on either cool or sunny days. The large bedrooms are nicely furnished with color-coordinated spreads, drapes, sofas and chairs. The dining room is especially attractive, a very large airy room with one solid wall of French doors which open out into a lakeview balcony with white wrought iron tables and chairs set for summer dining. Tennis enthusiasts will love the well kept courts. Although elegant, there is no stuffiness in this hotel. The staff are kind, friendly and gracious.

SCHLOSS SEEFELS
Owner: Constantin Dumba
Toschling 1, Portschach
Worthersee A-9210, Austria
Tel: (4272) 2377 Telex: 422153
75 Rooms - Dbl from AUS 1,100 to 3,500
Open: Dec 20 - Feb 29, Apr 15 - Oct 15
Credit cards: All major
U.S. Rep: David B. Mitchell
Rep tel: 800-372-1323
Located in southern Austria

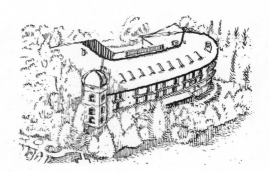

Sehr geehrte Herren,
Dear Sirs,

Wir (Ich) benotigen vom _____ _____ - 19__
We (I) wish to reserve as of   *day*   *month*   *year*   *(arrival date)*

           bis zum _____ _____ 19__
           until   *day*   *month*   year
                                     (departure date)

_____ Zimmer mit Bad / Dusche
           number of rooms with private bath / shower

_____ Zimmer mit Bad / Dusche am Gang,
           number of room(s) with bath / shower down the hall,

fur _____ Erwachsene mit _____ Kind(er).
for number of   *adults*   *with*   *number of children.*

Wir mochten:
We would like:

     ☐   nur Zimmer mit Frustuck
          room(s) with breakfast only

     ☐   mit Halbpension
          with breakfast and either lunch or dinner

     ☐   mit Vollpension
          with all meals

Bitte lassen Sie mich wissen, ob Sie etwas zu der gewunschten Zeit frei haben, in welcher Preislage, und ob Anzahlung notwendig ist.

Please let me know if you have a room available, in what price range and if a deposit is required.

Ich danke Ihnen im Voraus.
Thanking you in advance,

Mit freundlichen Grussen,
With friendly greetings,

ALPHABETICAL LISTING OF HOTELS BY HOTEL NAME

HOTEL	TOWN	Map Number	Page(s)

Index by Hotel Name

HOTEL	TOWN	Map Number		Page(s)
PLAINBRUCKE, GASTHOF ZUR	Salzburg	29		158
PLOMBERG-ESCHLBOCK, HOTEL	Mondsee-Plomberg	27	52,	149
POST, HOTEL	Lech	44		139
POST, HOTEL	Lofer	30		144
POST, HOTEL	Millstatt	19		147
POST, ROMANTIK HOTEL	Imst	41		126
POST, ROMANTIK HOTEL	Villach	17	88,	179
RAFFELSBERGERHOF	Weissenkirchen	8		182
RICHARD LOWENHERZ, HOTEL	Durnstein	7		112
ROMISCHER KAISER, ROMANTIK HOT.	Vienna	1		176
SACHER, HOTEL	Vienna	1		177
SCHLOSSBERG HOTEL	Graz	6		120
SCHLOSSWIRT, ROMANTIK HOTEL	Salzburg-Anif	29		161
SCHONEBEN, HOTEL	Wald im Pinzgau	32		181
SEEFELS, SCHLOSS	Worthersee-Portschach	16	42, 89,	187
SEEHOF, HOTEL	Goldegg am See	23		118
STADTKRUG, HOTEL	Salzburg	29		159
STERN, GASTHOF ZUM	Oetz	40		150
STRASSHOFER, HOTEL	Kitzbuhel	31		134
TENNE, HOTEL ZUR	Kitzbuhel	31		135
TENNERHOF, ROMANTIK HOTEL	Kitzbuhel	31	44,	136
TRAUBE, GASTHOF ZUR	Innsbruck-Lans	35		129
TRAUBE, ROMANTIK HOTEL	Lienz	20		141
TRUMER STUBERL, GASTHOF	Salzburg	29		160
WEISSEN ROSSL, HOTEL IM	St. Wolfgang	26		169
WIENER STAATSOPER, HOTEL ZUR	Vienna	1		178
ZAUNER, GASTHOF	Hallstatt	25	55,	123

Index by Hotel Name

ALPHABETICAL LISTING OF HOTELS BY TOWN NAME

Index by Town Name

TOWN	HOTEL	Map Number	Page(s)
ISCHGL	Gasthof Goldener Adler	42	132
KAPFENSTEIN	Schloss Kapfenstein	5	102, 133
KITZBUHEL	Hotel Strasshofer	31	134
KITZBUHEL	Hotel Zur Tenne	31	135
KITZBUHEL	Romantik Hotel Tennerhof	31	44, 136
KLAGENFURT	Romantik Hotel Musil	15	81, 137
LECH	Hotel Arlberg	44	74, 138
LECH	Hotel Post	44	139
LERMOOS	Hotel Drei Mohren	38	140
LIENZ	Romantik Hotel Traube	20	141
LOCKENHAUS	Burg Lockenhaus	3	142
LOFER	Hotel Brau	30	143
LOFER	Hotel Post	30	144
MAYRHOFEN	Hotel Garni Prem	34	145
MILLSTATT	Die Forelle Hotel	19	146
MILLSTATT	Hotel Post	19	147
MILLSTATT-OBERMILLSTATT	Alpenrose	19	83, 148
MONDSEE-PLOMBERG	Hotel Plomberg-Eschlbock	27	52, 149
OETZ	Gasthof Zum Stern	40	150
PERTISAU	Pension Enzian	36	151
SALZBURG	Gasthaus Zur Goldenen Ente	29	152
SALZBURG	Hotel Goldener Hirsch	29	153
SALZBURG	Pension Herbert	29	154
SALZBURG	Hotel Kasererbrau	29	155
SALZBURG	Schloss Monchstein	29	156
SALZBURG	Pension Nonntal	29	157
SALZBURG	Gasthof Zur Plainbrucke	29	158
SALZBURG	Hotel Stadtkrug	29	159

Index by Town Name

Index by Town Name

INN DISCOVERIES FROM OUR READERS

Future editions of *KAREN BROWN'S COUNTRY INN GUIDES TO EUROPE* are going to include a new feature - a list of hotels recommended by our readers. We have received many letters describing wonderful inns you have discovered; however, we have never included them until we had the opportunity to make a personal inspection. This seemed a waste of some marvelous "tips". Therefore, in order to feature them we have decided to add a new section called "Inn Discoveries from Our Readers".

If you have a favorite discovery you would be willing to share with other travelers who love to travel the "inn way", please let us hear from you and include the following information:

1. *Your name, address and telephone number.*

2. *Name, address and telephone number of "your inn".*

3. *Brochure or picture of inn (we cannot return material).*

4. *Written permission to use an edited version of your description.*

5. *Would you want your name, city and state included in the book?*

In addition to our current guide books, we are also researching future books in Europe and updating those previously published. We would appreciate comments on any of your favorites. The types of inns we would love to hear about are those with special "olde-worlde" ambiance, charm and atmosphere. We need a brochure or picture so that we can select those which most closely follow the mood of our guides. We look forward to hearing from you. Thank you.

Karen Brown's Country Inn Guides to Europe

The Most Reliable & Informative Series on European Country Inns

Detailed itineraries guide you through the countryside and suggest a cozy inn for each night's stay. In the hotel section, every listing has been inspected and chosen for its romantic ambiance. Charming accommodations reflect every price range, from budget hideaways to deluxe palaces.

Order Form

KAREN BROWN'S COUNTRY INN GUIDES TO EUROPE

Please ask in your local bookstore for KAREN BROWN'S COUNTRY INN guides. If the books you want are unavailable, you may order directly from the publisher.

AUSTRIAN COUNTRY INNS & CASTLES $12.95
ENGLISH, WELSH & SCOTTISH COUNTRY INNS $12.95
EUROPEAN COUNTRY CUISINE - ROMANTIC INNS & RECIPES $10.95
EUROPEAN COUNTRY INNS - BEST ON A BUDGET $14.95
FRENCH COUNTRY INNS & CHATEAUX $12.95
GERMAN COUNTRY INNS & CASTLES $12.95
IRISH COUNTRY INNS $12.95
ITALIAN COUNTRY INNS & VILLAS $12.95
PORTUGUESE COUNTRY INNS & POUSADAS $12.95
SCANDINAVIAN COUNTRY INNS & MANORS $12.95
SPANISH COUNTRY INNS & PARADORS $12.95
SWISS COUNTRY INNS & CHALETS $12.95

Name _____ *Street* _____
City _____ *State* _____ *Zip* _____

Add $2.00 per copy for postage & handling. California residents add sales tax.
Indicate the number of copies of each title. Send in form with your check to:

TRAVEL PRESS
P.O Box 70
San Mateo, CA 94401
(415) 342-9117

KAREN BROWN traveled to France in 1979 to write *French Country Inns & Chateaux* - the first book of what has grown to be an extremely successful series on European country inns. With 12 guides now on the market, Karen's staff has expanded, but she is still totally involved in planning, researching, formatting and editing each of her books. Karen loves to travel and returns frequently to Europe to investigate new hotels and to revisit familiar ones. Karen, her husband, Rick, and their daughter, Alexandra, live in the San Francisco Bay area.

CLARE BROWN, CTC, has many years of experience in the field of travel and has earned the designation of Certified Travel Consultant. Since 1969 she has specialized in planning itineraries to Europe using charming small hotels in the countryside for her clients. The focus of her job remains unchanged, but now her expertise is available to a larger audience - the readers of her daughter Karen's Country Inn guides. Clare lives in the San Francisco Bay area with her husband, Bill.

BARBARA TAPP, born in Sydney, Australia, where she studied at the School of Interior Design, is the talented artist responsible for the cover paintings and interior sketches for most of Karen Brown's Country Inn guides. Barbara lives in the San Francisco Bay area with her husband, Richard, their young sons, Jonathon and Alexander, and a new baby daughter, Georgia, who arrived the day Barbara was conscientiously finishing the last sketch for *Austrian Country Inns & Castles*.

This guide is especially written for the individual traveler who wants to plan his own vacation. However, should you prefer to join a group, Town and Country - Hillsdale Travel can recommend tours using country inns with romantic ambiance for many of the nights' accommodation. Or, should you want to organize your own group (art class, gourmet society, bridge club, church group, etc.) and travel with friends, custom tours can be arranged using small hotels with special charm and appeal. For further information please call:

Town & Country - Hillsdale Travel
16 East Third Avenue
San Mateo, California 94401

(415) 342-5591
Outside California 800-227-6733